# CLIMATE CHANGE AND SOCIETY

# Climate Change and Society
## Consequences of Increasing Atmospheric Carbon Dioxide
### William W. Kellogg and Robert Schware

As man's ability to disrupt the climate becomes increasingly apparent, evidence is mounting that human-activity–induced climate changes may well rival anything nature can produce. If the consensus of the international climatological community is correct, and if worldwide use of fossil fuel continues to increase atmospheric carbon dioxide, mankind is likely to cause a significant average warming of the Earth's surface—a greenhouse effect—within the next fifty years.

This book summarizes current knowledge of the causes of climatic change and presents a scenario of the future climate distribution that could prevail on a warmer Earth. It then focuses on the impacts of climatic change—in particular, a global warming accompanied by a shift in rainfall patterns—in such vital areas as food and fiber production, water resources, natural ecological systems, fisheries, health and disease, energy demand, and so forth.

The authors discuss in detail the political, economic, social, and ethical implications of global environmental change. They also evaluate national and international strategies for mitigating the impacts of climatic change or possibly averting that change altogether. Many of these strategies could be of immediate value in making agricultural and other climate-dependent systems more nearly "climate proof" now.

**William W. Kellogg** is a senior scientist at the National Center for Atmospheric Research (NCAR) and an architect of the World Climate Programme of the World Meteorological Organization. **Robert Schware** is a political scientist in the Advanced Study Program at NCAR. They wrote this book under the auspices of the Aspen Institute for Humanistic Studies, supported by a contract with the U.S. Department of Energy.

Published in Cooperation with the
Aspen Institute for Humanistic Studies
Program on Food, Climate and the World's Future
Boulder, Colorado

# CLIMATE CHANGE AND SOCIETY

## CONSEQUENCES OF INCREASING ATMOSPHERIC CARBON DIOXIDE

William W. Kellogg
and
Robert Schware

Westview Press / Boulder, Colorado

This book was prepared with the partial support of the U.S. Department of Energy, Contract No. DE-AC02-79EV10281. However, any opinions, findings, conclusions, and/or recommendations herein are those of the authors and do not necessarily reflect the views of the Department of Energy.

Published in 1981 in the United States of America by
  Westview Press, Inc.
  5500 Central Avenue
  Boulder, Colorado 80301
  Frederick A. Praeger, Publisher

Second printing, 1982

Library of Congress Card Catalog Number: 80-54157
ISBN: 0-86531-179-X; 0-86531-180-3 pb

Composition for this book was provided by the authors.

Printed and bound in the United States of America.

# CONTENTS

# FOREWORD

Human activity is rivaling nature's ability to produce climatic changes. Although there are large uncertainties in our knowledge of climate, many climatologists now believe that future climates will differ significantly from those of today. The primary reason: our steady contribution to the atmospheric burden of carbon dioxide, produced largely through fossil fuel use and possibly through deforestation. There is a growing world concern that this carbon dioxide buildup will lead to a global warming without precedent in human history. It is quite possible that this so-called "greenhouse effect" will dominate within the next 50 years. If so, we can expect major alterations of regional rainfall and temperature patterns; their magnitude and timing, however, are uncertain.

Climate variability is one of the largest stumbling blocks to stable agricultural production. Food supplies are vulnerable to climatic anomalies and occasional "abnormal" weather. Moreover, climate fluctuations often accelerate the degradation of natural forest lands, increase wind and water erosion of productive agricultural and grazing soils, and heighten the effects of overgrazing and desertification. These short term impacts constitute a serious threat to our ability to sustain increasing world populations. A climatic change could make things worse.

Clearly, this prospect of a major environmental change presages globally important social, economic, political, and ethical issues. But we wish to make it clear that we do not consider the occurrence of a greenhouse warming a certainty. Our aim in conducting this year-long study has been to suggest ways to refine our understanding of the impact of a possible climate change upon societies, examine the issues that might arise, and make a preliminary evaluation of alternative strategies for mitigating the effects or averting the change.

Many of the long term strategies designed to deal with a climate warming would also make agricultural and other social systems more nearly "climate proof" now. They can guard against the adverse effects of the normal short term climate fluctuations, giving added insurance in the event of a long term climate change. If the public perceives these benefits clearly, then implementing the strategies may be more politically acceptable.

The idea for the Aspen Institute study was originated by the Climate Program of the International Federation of Institutes for Advanced Study (IFIAS). At a 1974 workshop at the University of Bonn IFIAS members proposed conducting a study of the implications of a hypothetical climate change. Subsequently, another workshop was held at the Aspen Institute in Colorado in October 1978. It was co-sponsored by the World Meteorological Organization (WMO) and the United Nations Environment Programme (UNEP). With the enthusiastic help of Mr. David Slade of the Department of Energy's Carbon Dioxide Effects Research and Assessment Program, a group of experts at this workshop further explored the prospects of a carbon dioxide-induced warming. They recommended this one-year study.

The Department of Energy became the principal sponsor of our project. Additional support has come from the Weyerhaeuser Foundation, the Volkswagen Foundation, the Mitre Corporation, the National Center for Atmospheric Research (sponsored by the National Science Foundation), and the Aspen Institute for Humanistic Studies in Berlin and in this country.

Our study team was headed by Dr. William W. Kellogg, a meteorologist and senior scientist at the National Center for Atmospheric Research. He took a half time leave of absence to direct the study. Dr. Robert Schware, a political scientist, assumed full time responsibility as study co-author; and I gave overall guidance.

The project's Steering Committee, which helped tremendously, also actively participated in the project. Members of this committee are: Representative George Brown, Jr., U.S. Congress; Dr. Rolando Garcia, Universidad Autonoma, Mexico; Dr. Stanley M. Greenfield, Teknekron, Inc.; Dr. Robert W. Kates, Clark University; Dr. Lester Lave, Brookings Institution; Dr. Donella Meadows, Dartmouth College; Dr. Mihajlo Mesarovic, Case Western Reserve University; Dr. V. Kerry Smith, University of North Carolina; Dr. Edith Brown Weiss, Georgetown University Law Center; Dr. Gilbert F. White, University of Colorado; and Dr. Robert M. White, President, University Corporation for Atmospheric Research.

Some of these Steering Committee members participated in the project's two workshops. The first was held in February 1980 at the Aspen Institute's Wye Plantation in Maryland; the second at the Aspen Institute in Berlin in May 1980. The latter was co-sponsored by the WMO and IFIAS; it included a distinguished group of scientists and statesmen from both Europe and developing countries.

The evolutionary approach by the authors to the preparation of this report was somewhat unusual. The first thing they did was to write an abbreviated "first draft" of the entire report, which they discussed personally with each member of the Steering Committee early in December. The Wye Workshop in February was devoted to a discussion of their outline of a National Program on Assessment of Economic, Social, and Political Impacts of Carbon Dioxide–Induced Climatic Change, which was designed to help the Department of Energy in its organization of such a program and also to bring out important issues for debate. A "second draft" of the full report was prepared prior to the Berlin Workshop in May, and not only served as the agenda for that meeting but was also used for further discussions with some members of the Steering Committee and others. With all this background they then turned to drafting this final report.

In February 1979 scientists attending the World Climate Conference, organized by the World Meteorological Organization in Geneva, expressed strong concern over the international implications of the "carbon dioxide problem" and future climate changes. As a result the WMO's World Climate Programme was created. One of its mandates is to assess, in collaboration with the UNEP, the social and economic impacts of climatic variability and change. It is our hope that this study will assist future impact assessment efforts, including specifically those sponsored by the U.S. National Climate Program.

Boulder, Colorado                    Walter Orr Roberts, Director
                                     Program on Food, Climate and
                                                the World's Future,
                             Aspen Institute for Humanistic Studies

# ACKNOWLEDGEMENTS

We are indebted to many individuals for generous contributions of time, creative effort, and expertise. Special mention should be made of Dr. Edward J. Friedman of the Mitre Corporation, some of whose work on past and future energy and fossil fuel use is incorporated here; and Dr. Lester B. Lave, of the Brookings Institution, a part of whose special report on mitigating strategies has also been incorporated. Ms. Randi S. Londer has been our Editorial Assistant and provided invaluable help during the writing of the final draft.

Among those who have read and provided detailed comments on our various drafts (in addition to members of the Steering Committee named in the Foreword) are Dr. Michael H. Glantz, Dr. Stephen H. Schneider, Dr. Stella Melugin Coakley, Dr. Gordon A. McKay, Prof. Wilfrid Bach, Dr. H. Le Houérou, Dr. Alexander King, and Dr. Pierre Spitz. We have also obtained a great many inputs from all those who participated in the two Aspen Institute meetings, whose names are listed below.

The effort could never have succeeded without the ministerings of Mary Wolff, Associate Director of Aspen's Project on Food, Climate and the World's Future, assisted in the early stages by Ms. Marita Melaugh and in the later stages by Ms. Violet M. Mills. Special thanks must go to the people who patiently and expertly typed and retyped our drafts, especially Ms. Mary F. Rickel and Ms. Eileen Boettner; and to Mr. William E. Hemphill of NCAR, who was in charge of our drafting, and Mr. Charles G. Semmer, who did the photographic processing of figures.

The following participated in the Workshop at Aspen Institute's Wye Plantation, Maryland, 25–29 February 1980:

Dr. Arnold Baker, Atlantic Richfield Co.
Prof. Donald Borock, Gettysburg College
Mr. David M. Burns, American Association for the Advancement of Science
Prof. Ralph C. d'Arge, University of Wyoming
Mr. Walter Hahn, Congressional Research Service, Library of Congress

Dr. William W. Kellogg, Aspen Institute and National Center for Atmospheric Research

Dr. Lester B. Lave, Brookings Institution

Mr. Howard Lewis, Director of Public Information, National Academy of Sciences

Prof. Donella Meadows, Resource Policy Center, Dartmouth College

Prof. Mihajlo Mesarovic, Case Western Reserve University

Dr. Thomas H. Moss, Staff of Congressman George Brown

Dr. John S. Perry, Climate Research Board, National Academy of Sciences

Mr. Chester L. Parsons, Aspen Institute and NASA Wallops Island Flight Center

Mr. Frank M. Potter, Jr., Staff Director and Counsel, Subcommittee on Energy and Power, Committee on Interstate and Foreign Commerce, U.S. House of Representatives

Dr. Walter Orr Roberts, Aspen Institute

Dr. Robert Schware, Aspen Institute

Prof. V. Kerry Smith, University of North Carolina

Mr. Walter Sullivan, *The New York Times*

Dr. Charles Weiss, International Bank for Reconstruction and Development

Prof. Gilbert F. White, Institute of Behavioral Science, University of Colorado

Mr. Thomas W. Wilson, Jr., Writer and Consultant, Washington, D.C.

## Government Liaison Representatives

Mr. Roger Dahlman, Department of Energy

Dr. Pamela Kacser, Department of Energy

Dr. Harry Moses, Department of Energy

Mr. David Slade, Department of Energy

Dr. Thomas Waltz, National Climate Program Office

The following participated in the Workshop at Aspen Institute's West Berlin Conference Center, 18–22 May 1980. We wish first to express our special appreciation to Dr. Shepard Stone, Director of Aspen Institute Berlin, and Mr. James Cooney, who made the excellent local arrangements for the meeting and helped in many aspects of its organization:

Dr. Clement Dorm Adzobu, Visiting Fellow from Ghana, International Institute for Environment and Society, Berlin

Prof. Wilfrid Bach, University of Münster

Dr. Reinier Braams, Member of Parliament, Utrecht, Netherlands

Mr. David M. Burns, American Association for the Advancement of Science, Washington, D.C.

Dr. Roberto Fantechi, Commission of the European Communities Brussels

Dr. Laila El-Hamamsy, UN Research Institute for Social Development, Geneva

Dr. Siegfried Hantzsch, Senate for Health and Environment, Berlin

Dr. Gerrit P. Hekstra, Ministry of Public Health and the Environment, Leidschendam, Netherlands

Dr. H. Le Houérou, International Livestock Center for Africa, Addis Ababa

Dr. Stuart Jenks, Free University of Berlin

Dr. William Kellogg, Aspen Institute and National Center for Atmospheric Research, Boulder

Dr. Alexander King, International Federation of Institutes for Advanced Study, Paris

Dr. Gundolf Kohlmeier, University of Frankfurt

Dr. Cesare Marchetti, International Institute for Applied Systems Analysis, Laxenburg, Austria

Dr. A.C. Mascarenhas, University of Dar-Es-Salaam, Tanzania

Dr. Rashmi Mayur, Urban Development Institute, Bombay

Prof. Klaus M. Meyer-Abich, University of Essen, F.R.G.

Prof. Richard S. Odingo, United Nations University, Tokyo

Mr. Jurgen Pankrath, Federal Environmental Agency, Berlin

Dr. Giancarlo Pinchera, Italian Energy Commission, Rome

Prof. Amos Richmond, Ben Gurion University, Sede-Boqer, Israel

Dr. Walter Orr Roberts, Aspen Institute, Boulder

Dr. Gottfried Schnatz, Batelle Institute, Frankfurt

Dr. Robert Schware, Aspen Institute, Boulder

Dr. Willem Smit, International Energy Agency, Paris

Dr. Pierre Spitz, UN Research Institute for Social Development, Geneva

Dr. C.C. Wallen, Global Environmental Monitoring System/UN Environment Programme, Geneva

**Observers**

Dr. Meinolf Dierkes, International Institute for Environment & Society, Berlin

Mr. Alejandro Spitzy, University of Hamburg (Representing SCOPE)

Mr. Key Landmann-Ulrich, *International Environment Reporter*, Bonn

William W. Kellogg
Robert Schware

# OVERVIEW

## Introduction

If the consensus of the international climatological community is correct, and if world fossil fuel use continues to increase atmospheric carbon dioxide, mankind will likely cause a significant average warming of the Earth's surface within the next 50 years.

However, for planning and management purposes it is not very useful just to know that a climatic change is in store. The political, economic, social, and ethical implications of a global environmental change must be considered. In this report, we address these issues and suggest some potential strategies to deal with the carbon dioxide problem.

We have also tried to cull references that will give readers an idea of the kinds of research being done on climate related problems; many disciplines are involved in trying to better understand the impacts that a warmer Earth will have on human activities. Even though the academic establishment encourages specialization, the carbon dioxide problem is so complex it requires a multidisciplinary approach to clarify the issues and assess strategies. Hence, a climatic impact study program must extend communication between meteorologists, oceanographers, geographers, political scientists, economists, psychologists, and engineers, among others.

It is our hope that much of the material we present can be used as a guide for those who will undertake future climatic impact studies, and a background document for policy makers who are in a position to implement specific strategies that might mitigate the adverse effects of climatic change — or possibly even avert the change.

A strong incentive exists for implementing these strategies: it turns out that they may increase each nation's resilience to short term climatic variations as well as long term climatic changes. This may make our agricultural and other systems less vulnerable to the vagaries of climate and also prepare us for an altered climate in the future. Hence, these measures should be adopted in any case. Perhaps the issue of carbon dioxide-induced climate change will serve as a stimulus to employ such strategies sooner. Many of them are long overdue.

1

## Carbon Dioxide and Climatic Change

While this report emphasizes the societal impacts of a carbon dioxide-induced change, we recognize that is is important to understand the possible nature of that change. Climate research is devoted to gaining more knowledge of the physical basis of climate and of climatic change. This includes the influence of human activities on the Earth-atmosphere-ocean system that determines the climate. Climate research is being pursued by many scientists and research organizations in the United States and abroad; it is organized internationally under the World Climate Research Programme, which is jointly sponsored by the World Meteorological Organization and the International Council of Scientific Unions.

The research can be divided into three main areas. Scientists are studying:

- *The physical changes of the Earth's surface and atmospheric composition, both of which can influence the behavior of the climate system.* Since the beginning of the Industrial Revolution, the increasing use of fossil fuels (coal, petroleum, natural gas) has added to the atmospheric burden of carbon dioxide. It is a trace gas that now constitutes about 0.034 percent of the atmosphere; this concentration is estimated to be 15 to 20 percent higher than it was at the turn of the century. Predicting its future rise depends on having good estimates of: the fraction of the added carbon dioxide that will remain in the air; the fraction that will be taken up by the oceans; the fraction that will be taken up or released by living biota (especially the tropical forests); and future patterns of fossil fuel use. The last is the most difficult to predict, since it depends on the future energy policies of all countries. It is reasonable to expect that the concentration of carbon dioxide could be 30 to 50 percent higher than its pre-1900 value by the year 2000, and that it will be double that value around the middle of the next century. Of course, a successful effort to reduce the burning of fossil fuels could delay the doubling time. This could be achieved by widespread energy conservation and use of alternative energy sources that do not release carbon dioxide to the atmosphere.

- *The effects of increased carbon dioxide on climate.* Carbon dioxide is a trace gas that is virtually transparent to sunlight. But it absorbs part of the infrared radiation that is emitted upwards by the Earth's surface. As a result the lower atmosphere and the Earth's surface are warmer than they would otherwise be. This is

2

the so-called "greenhouse effect", and as the concentration of carbon dioxide increases, this effect will make the surface still warmer.

The radiative effects of carbon dioxide are well understood; the other changes that may occur in the atmosphere, oceans, and ice masses of the polar regions (called the "cryosphere") are less well understood. Experiments with theoretical models of the climate system indicate that the average global increase of surface temperature for a doubling of carbon dioxide will probably be between 1.5°C and 4.5°C. Warming in the Antarctic will be somewhat greater, and it will be two or three times larger in the Arctic. There will be significant shifts in the global atmospheric and oceanic circulation patterns, which together determine regional temperature and precipitation.

There is good reason to believe that a warming of the polar regions will cause the massive ice sheets of the Antarctic and Greenland to shrink, or perhaps to slide into the ocean more rapidly than they do now. A disintegration of even a portion of the ice sheets, such as the part in West Antarctica that could become unstable, would cause sea level to rise by several meters. However, glaciologists cannot agree on what time scale this would occur.

● *Illustrating the range of possible future climates by climate scenarios.* What policy makers and planners need is a description of plausible long term changes of average temperature, precipitation, evaporation, and soil moisture on a *regional* and *seasonal* scale. It would also be useful to know the short term variability of these weather factors, since the occasional occurrence of extreme events such as droughts, heat waves, cold spells, blizzards, and floods are clearly significant. However, climatologists cannot yet agree on the details of the climate of a future warmer Earth.

Hence, the next best thing is to provide climate "scenarios" — a set of descriptions, probably in the form of seasonal maps, showing the *range of conditions* that could plausibly occur. Scenarios should be based on all available evidence, including results of climate model experiments and studies of past climate changes. They should not be considered as predictions, but rather as likely examples that can be used to explore the impacts of climatic changes, and as a basis from which to develop alternative strategies to mitigate the adverse impacts.

For instance, one scenario that we have drawn indicates how soil moisture during the growing season in a warmer Earth may deviate from the present. The midwestern U.S. will be drier, Europe and North Africa wetter, and the Soviet Union and northern China drier, according to this scenario. Such scenarios should obviously be extended and improved as we learn more about the causes of climate change.

## Impacts of Climatic Change

The World Climate Programme, established in 1979 by the World Meteorological Organization (WMO), has as one of its goals defining climatic variability and change in terms of what they mean for societies.

In the past few decades short term weather anomalies and slowly developing changes of climate have triggered severe economic, social, and political dislocations. In the 1970s adverse weather in a few regions affected food prices, balance of trade, and human settlements worldwide. Developed and developing countries alike find themselves increasingly vulnerable to "abnormal weather". Furthermore, there is a growing realization that a carbon dioxide–induced climatic change could have much larger impacts than any of these short term events.

Studying such climatic impacts is already an established practice. Water resource managers consider climate in their planning; agronomists use crop models to predict changes in productivity for given changes in temperature, precipitation, and sunlight; economists have been experimenting with models that attempt to forecast the costs and benefits of a specified climatic change on certain economic sectors; and anthropologists have long been aware of the effects of climate on patterns of migration and settlement. What appears to be new about climatic impact studies is the attempt to take into account many factors, all dealing specifically with the carbon dioxide/climate problem.

We have looked at the potential impacts on several climate sensitive activities. These include:

● *Energy supply and demand.* The largest single use of energy in the temperate latitudes of the industrialized world is for space heating and cooling; this is markedly influenced by temperature variations. Energy is also needed in many areas, such as California and the western Great Plains, for pumping water for irrigation; during dry years, more is needed.

The winter of 1976–77, for example, was characterized by a simultaneous cold spell in the eastern half of the United States and a drought in the western half, including a very dry "rainy season"

4

in California. The result was an estimated $20 billion in energy related losses to the U.S. gross national product that year due to excess energy usage and loss of productivity.

There are other sectors, such as transportation and tourism, whose energy demands are affected by climate. However, it is often hard to separate the effects of climate variations from the other economic and social factors involved.

Energy supply is also affected by climate, as in the case of that same cold winter of 1976–77. In the eastern United States oil and coal barges were ice bound, piles of coal were too frozen to move, and natural gas storage areas required more pumping due to a decrease of pressure. The fuel shortages accounted for an estimated one million unemployed by February 1977. However, part of this shortage was due to the fact that the utility and pipeline companies neglected to plan ahead and store fuel reserves. Although the following winter (1977–78) was almost as severe, they were then much better prepared to meet the extra demand.

There is a current move to replace centralized fossil fuel and nuclear power sources with renewable sources such as hydroelectric, solar, wind, and biomass. Though this may be desirable, it will tend to make our energy supplies more sensitive to the vagaries of the climate, depending as they do on rainfall, sunshine, and steady winds.

Energy demand in the tropics would probably change little if global temperatures rose due to an increase in carbon dioxide. However, at middle latitudes there would be a decrease of demand for heating in the winter and an increase in demand for air conditioning in summer, shifting the kind of power from heating fuel to electricity. The pattern of energy demands will not shift uniformly poleward, since, as we have emphasized, the regional changes of temperature and rainfall will be complex.

- *World food production.* Some aspects of the projected climatic changes due to carbon dioxide could be beneficial for crops and other ecosystems, depending on where they are growing. More carbon dioxide is known to enhance photosynthesis and plant growth. A 1°C rise in average summertime temperatures at middle latitudes increases the average growing season by roughly ten days, an obvious advantage. The increase of precipitation in the semiarid regions of the subtropics called for in our scenario could also be advantageous.

Of course, every food crop responds differently to a given climatic change. For several major food crops the relationships

5

between climate and productivity are fairly well known. But for other crops, particularly those grown in the subtropics, further study is still needed.

Equally important to food production may be the changing climate's effects on the frequency and severity of pest outbreaks. Currently, agricultural losses due to pests are about 25 percent. Thus, a temperature increase may make pest control even more difficult than it already is. The same may be true for a number of plant diseases, such as stripe rust on winter wheat.

Even though agricultural technology has given us hardy crop strains, many experts believe that the monoculture we depend on for food is so specialized that it is far more vulnerable to climatic variations and change than the natural ecosystems it replaced. It should be noted that 95 percent of human nutrition is derived from no more than 30 different kinds of plants; just three crops — wheat, rice, and maize — account for over 75 percent of our cereal production. A 1972 National Academy of Sciences report (entitled "The Genetic Vulnerability of Crops") states that the crop varieties grown in the United States are "impressively uniform genetically and impressively vulnerable."

In principle we can use new crop varieties that are better adapted to a changed climate. But plant geneticists are concerned about the rapidly decreasing stocks of vigorous wild strains and disease resistant food crops; these are being pushed out as their natural ecosystems are damaged or eliminated.

● *Global ecology.* While agricultural systems may depend on a few specialized plant species, natural ecosystems — or "biomes" — are usually characterized by a great diversity of plants and animals. These organisms interact and live together in an intricate balance — that is, until this balance is disturbed by humans or by climatic change. Few biomes, if any, remain untouched by human influence. Among the major biomes that are still close to their original states are the remote tropical forests that have not yet been exploited, and the unpopulated tundra areas of the Arctic.

The kind of biome that will thrive in a given region is determined by temperature, precipitation, soil type, and availability of sunlight, among other variables. The first two are generally the most important. A slow climatic change will affect temperature and precipitation, forcing the biomes to shift, as some species in each region die out and others succeed them. This has occurred many times throughout geological history. For example, during the warm Altithermal Period some 5000 years ago the spruce forests of central Canada extended 300 to 400 kilometers further north than they do now. At that time the Sahara was not a desert but a semiarid grassland that supported grazing animals and nomadic people.

Whether ecosystems can adapt successfully to a climatic change will depend on how fast the change occurs. This is because, while the life span of individual trees and other plants is many decades, the response of an entire ecosystem occurs over several plant lifetimes.

A special biome exists in the Arctic tundra, where few trees grow and permafrost (permanently frozen ground) inhibits drainage, slowing the decay of dead plants. The result is the accumulation of deep layers of water saturated or frozen organic matter, called peat. If there is a general warming trend — and recall that the warming is expected to be greatest in the Arctic — permafrost will gradually retreat northward, trees will encroach on what had been tundra, and the peat bogs will thaw and dry out in their upper layers. As a result, the upper layers of organic matter will oxidize once they become exposed to the air for the first time. This will probably produce carbon dioxide and add further to the warming — an example of a "positive feedback."

Hence, a gradual climate change will cause the distribution of biomes to shift as each seeks to adapt and achieve a new equilibrium. These shifts are fairly predictable, provided that natural processes alone are involved. However, in many parts of the world human intervention will have a larger ecological impact than the shifting climate in the next 50 to 100 years.

- *Water resources.* We depend on a reliable supply of fresh water for survival. A climate change will surely shift patterns of precipitation, and this will directly affect the water resources of every region. Areas with marginal water resources will be the hardest hit if there is a decrease in rainfall; our tentative scenario indicates such areas in the midwestern United States and the Soviet Union.

  Currently many developing countries in the semiarid parts of the subtropics are now expected to experience a general increase of precipitation and soil moisture if a climate warming occurs. Changes in precipitation and soil moisture are key elements in food and forest production. Hence, the climatic warming could perhaps adversely affect the two "superpowers" and help a great many developing countries.

7

Many of the dams, aqueducts, pumping stations, reservoirs, and water distribution networks around the world have been designed to cope with seasonal and year-to-year fluctuations of water supply and demand. The lifetime of such facilities is typically 50 to 100 years or more, so the anticipated climatic change will occur while they are still in place. Whether they will still be adequate is in question.

In any case, any measures taken now to guarantee more reliable water supplies will be advantageous regardless of longer term climatic changes. Even without a future shift of precipitation patterns they will probably be cost effective.

● *Fisheries.* Up until the early 1970s rivers, lakes, and coastal areas of the world were generally viewed as vast, almost limitless resources of food. As late as the 1960s and early 1970s scientists had reported that fish catches could be greatly increased, and would provide a large supplement to food production on land. However, after 1972 global fish catches declined from their peak of 26.5 million tons to 18.5 million tons in 1973, according to the U.N. Food and Agriculture Organization. There has recently been a partial recovery, but not to the levels attained in the early 1970s.

Decreases in fish landings can be caused by a number of factors, either singly or in combination. These factors include overfishing, poor fishery management practices, and oceanographic and climatic fluctuations or changes. In 1972 and 1973 climatic fluctuations resulted in shifting ocean currents, sea surface temperatures, and wind patterns that may have been partly responsible for the general reduction in fish landings, and specifically in Peruvian coastal waters. The anchovy population there depends on an upwelling of nutrient rich cold deep water to the surface. In 1972 and 1973 a phenomenon called the El Niño — an invasion of warm, nutrient poor, surface water — depleted the nutrient supply and caused anchovies to die or disperse. There are other coastal zones that depend on upwelling to provide nutrients to the fish population; all are subject to similar year-to-year fluctuations of currents and water temperatures.

Another example of the influence of climate on fish catches is the West Greenland cod supply. Up to about 1950 North Atlantic temperatures increased, and during this period the catch also increased, reaching a peak of some 450,000 tons in the early 1960s. However, since then there has been a cooling trend, and in recent years catches of cod have been so low that they have been banned off Greenland.

While there seems to be good reason to believe that winds, temperatures, and ocean currents all play a part in determining the favorable environments for fish, the marine ecosystem is still poorly understood. It is difficult to separate the climatic impact from the human influence, such as overfishing. In any case, it appears that the sea is not so bountiful a source of food as once believed.

- *Health, comfort, and disease.* Human beings can survive environments from extremely hot (50°C) to extremely cold (–60°C). However, most people thrive best in a temperature range known as the "comfort zone", ranging a few degrees above or below the optimum of about 20°C. Very low or very high temperatures can negatively influence personal functions, motivation, and social behavior. One study has shown that temperate latitude workers become 2 to 4 percent less productive for every degree centigrade rise of temperature above the optimum. This explains why such workers are sluggish on hot days, especially when humidity is high. This point should be kept in mind when considering the impact of a general warming.

The prevalence of most diseases is also affected by climate, demonstrated by the seasonal outbreaks of certain illnesses in temperate regions and the limitations of other diseases to certain climatic zones in the tropics. Some human diseases depend on insects, snails, or other "vectors" for their spread, which are subject to temperature, moisture, and other climatic constraints.

But diseases are not solely linked to climate, since they are also affected by the condition of water supplies, food sanitation, and refuse disposal. Not surprisingly, most of the serious diseases are disproportionately concentrated in the poor and developing countries of the world, nations which tend to be in the tropics or subtropics. In short, poverty provides favorable conditions for the spread of disease, which also helps to perpetuate poverty.

In a global warming a number of diseases that are now mostly confined to the tropics might spread to more temperate regions. These diseases include schistosomiasis, bacillary dysentery, hookworms, yaws, and malaria. However, they could be eradicated by hygienic and other measures, so their spread is by no means inevitable.

- *Populations settlements.* Many population shifts have been at least partly due to an adverse climate. The emigration to the U.S. and Britain during the Irish Potato Famine in 1845 to 1851, and the abandonment of farms in Kansas, Texas, and Oklahoma during the 1930s Dust Bowl are two examples. Of course, the latter was triggered by abnormally low rainfall and high temperatures in the high plains, but poor grazing and plowing practices were a contributing factor. The drought of the 1950s in the same region did not cause as much disruption.

The developing world, which will probably contain more than three-quarters of the world population by 2000, is especially vulnerable to the pressures of climatic variations and change. The Sahelian disaster of 1968-1973, when over 100,000 North African nomads died, illustrates this point.

If a climatic warming caused sea level to rise, as we have mentioned, the densely populated coastal regions would face serious consequences. One study of what would happen with a 5 meter rise of sea level indicates that in the United States alone about 11 million people would be affected; that is 6 percent of the 1970 population. In Florida some 40 percent of the population would have to move. While these figures apply to the United States, it is obvious that a sea level rise would affect all coastal areas of the world.

It must be emphasized that glaciologists do not agree on the time scale for such an event, whose primary cause will be the shrinking or breakup of part of the great ice sheets of Greenland or Antarctica. The West Antarctic ice sheet has attracted the most attention, since it sits largely on bedrock below sea level, but whether it would disintegrate in a matter of decades, centuries, or millenia following a major warming is still being debated.

Thus, while it is clearly too early to make evacuation plans, we can begin to prepare for this contingency by applying what we know about land use and flooding in areas where water levels are already rising. For example, land is subsiding or shifting in Venice, Italy; Long Beach, California; and Galveston, Texas. This creates an apparent sea level rise for non-climatic reasons.

- *Tourism and recreation.* An increasing number of communities, and even entire countries, are becoming dependent on the income from tourism. It is an important economic sector that is also remarkably sensitive to climatic variations and change. The best example of this is a ski resort without adequate snowfall.

Health through recreation is becoming more popular throughout the world — that is, where people can afford the luxury of recreation. Climatic change will clearly affect the development of vacation facilities.

## Policy Decisions and Measures Dealing with the Carbon Dioxide/Climate Problem

### Long range strategies

While there are many long range strategies that can increase our resilience to climatic variability and change there are also certain obstacles to accepting and implementing them. Among these obstacles are the following:

- *Incomplete information.* Since climatologists still cannot predict with certainty future temperature and precipitation changes, either regionally or seasonally, it is not surprising that policy makers and the public are reluctant to commit resources to long range measures in order to mitigate a situation that might never occur. People prefer the "wait and see" attitude — wait for scientific information and see what happens if it does not materialize.

- *Poor planning and information distribution.* Climatological information, though available in archives, has not been properly consulted in a number of well documented cases. This seems to have been due to a lack of awareness on the part of the public and its planners of the opportunity and need for taking such information into account. The World Climate Data and Applications Programmes of the World Meteorological Organization are specifically designed to help countries organize their climate data and to make better use of knowledge about the climate.

- *Discounting the future.* When weighing risks and benefits there is the tendency to opt for near term gratification rather than longer term rewards. This tendency is especially strong when dealing with benefits to be reaped by future generations. What is their future worth to us today? Residents of flood plains, for instance, have denied the possibility of another flood occurring — at least, in their lifetime. This irrational discounting of the future often serves to their disadvantage, and governments as well as individuals can fall into the same trap. The same is true for carbon dioxide. Are we willing to accept the future risk of added carbon dioxide to the atmosphere for the present benefit of burning fossil fuels?

11

## Averting the change

This could involve stopping, or at least greatly reducing, fossil fuel use, removing carbon dioxide from combustion products before they reach the atmosphere, and by increasing the natural sinks of carbon dioxide. To have a significant effect these measures will have to be adopted by virtually all countries, since action by one or two nations alone will have little influence on the global buildup of carbon dioxide. These various possibilities are explored below.

- *Reduce fossil fuel demand.* Besides the rising cost of energy, the carbon dioxide/climate problem provides an additional incentive to reduce fossil fuel use. Energy conservation in developed countries is an obvious way to achieve this reduction. From the climatic point of view, replacing fossil fuels with renewable energy resources is also attractive. Nuclear energy is another alternative, since it does not produce carbon dioxide, but there is opposition to the increased use of nuclear power because of its health and environmental risks. However, energy conservation is a controversial point for developing countries. These nations are striving to build their industries or merely struggling to survive — indeed, energy conservation has little meaning for these countries when per capita energy consumption is, say, only 5 percent of that in the United States.

- *Technical solutions.* There are a number of imaginative technological proposals to decrease carbon dioxide emissions. Removing the gas at its source, namely, from the exhaust stacks of electric power plants, is one of them. This can be accomplished by running the gases through chemical collectors that selectively remove the carbon dioxide. The gas can then be separated from the collector so that the device can be reused. But this process requires a considerable expenditure of energy and capital.

  The next step in the proposed process is to transport the carbon dioxide to a suitable dumping site in the ocean (at a further expenditure of energy) where it will be transported downward by currents and mixed with bottom water. Since it probably takes several centuries for bottom water to mix with the rest of the ocean and return to the surface, this method will delay the final release of the carbon dioxide by that amount of time. There are variations on this idea such as running the stack gases directly into sea water, or pumping the gas back down into old gas wells. But so far the costs for facilities and extra energy appear to be enormous, rendering these solutions unattractive.

In a somewhat different category are the proposals to remove carbon dioxide from the atmosphere using non–fossil fuel power, such as nuclear, hydro, or solar power. The carbon dioxide would then be reduced by chemical processing together with heat and water to produce organic gases or liquids, like methane or heavier hydrocarbons. This can, in principle, provide synthetic fuels that will substitute for fossil fuels; they will recycle carbon dioxide rather than generate more. However, here again the costs would be enormous in terms of manpower, materials, and energy.

● *Increase biomass.* Plants take carbon dioxide out of the atmosphere through respiration and photosynthesis. When they die and decay, or are burned, the carbon returns to the atmosphere as carbon dioxide. Before human intervention this exchange must have nearly balanced out, but no longer. Extensive deforestation has destroyed the equilibrium and is causing the forests of the world, which constitute roughly 90 percent of the biosphere, to become another source of carbon dioxide, although exactly how much is debated.

It has been estimated that if global biomass is increased by 1 percent each year, then enough carbon will be absorbed to nearly equal the current release of $5 \times 10^9$ tons per year. But as a long term solution to the carbon dioxide problem reforestation by itself will be ineffective (though useful for other reasons). For one thing, with the current 4 percent yearly rate of increase of fossil fuel burning carbon dioxide production will double after only 17 years; to keep pace we would have to add 2 percent per year to the biomass. This is probably an unreasonably large effort, even if there were enough available land for all those trees.

Another way to deal with carbon dioxide is to cut down trees and sequester their carbon in old coal mines, caves, or the deep ocean. This prevents or at least delays their decay and the return of their carbon dioxide to the atmosphere. A more constructive alternative is to convert biomass to liquid fuels as a substitute for fossil fuels, which is already being tried in several countries. But this is still far out–stripped by fossil fuel production, and a large capital outlay and a new transportation infrastructure are needed to handle the wood if this scheme is to work. In short, reforestation and biomass conversion are measures that make sense for several reasons, but they are unlikely to be the solution to the carbon dioxide/climate problem.

## Mitigating the Effects

Regardless of whether carbon dioxide builds up and results in a future climatic change, problems caused by weather and climate variability occur now and will continue to do so. Thus, we should strive to reduce the vulnerability of human settlements and activities. As it turns out, a variety of long range strategies to mitigate the impacts of future climatic change would be wise steps to take for more immediate problems. Therefore these strategies should be implemented in any case.

We have identified three classes of long range strategies with short term benefits: those that increase resilience (or decrease vulnerability) to climatic change; those that help to reduce carbon dioxide emissions; and those that lead to making better choices.

## Strategies that increase resilience to climate change

- *Protect arable soil.* Agriculture and animal husbandry depend on soil that can grow plants. This resource is being poorly managed and lost through erosion and salinization. One of the world's most pressing environmental problems, it threatens our ability to produce enough food.

- *Improve water management.* Societies will continue to depend on water supply systems that can ameliorate floods and provide water during periods of drought.

- *Apply agrotechnology.* New agricultural techniques led to the "Green Revolution", and they may help us provide food for a growing population in the face of adverse climatic events and longer term climatic change.

- *Improve coastal land use policies.* Coastal communities need to make better use of climatic information to mitigate the effects of floods, hurricanes, and typhoons. A future sea level rise is one more factor that should be a part of their planning, even though its time scale is still uncertain.

- *Maintain global food reserves.* Future shifts of temperatures and precipitation patterns will affect some for the better, some for the worse. Thus, global food reserves to help the losers are a sound policy, both now and in the future.

- *Provide disaster relief.* Catastrophes will still require emergency aid from international relief organizations to alleviate their impact.

## Strategies that help reduce carbon dioxide emissions

- *Conserve energy.* There are strong incentives to make energy conservation the basis for a sound energy policy, since it reduces the demand for all fuels, including those from fossil sources.

- *Use renewable energy resources.* By the same token, use of renewable energy resources, such as solar energy, biomass conversion, and hydroelectric power will reduce the demand for fossil fuels.

- *Reforest.* Replanting trees in areas where deforestation has taken place, as in many parts of the tropics, not only replaces a valuable economic resource and prevents soil erosion, but also takes some carbon dioxide out of the atmosphere as the trees grow.

## Strategies that lead to improved choices

- *Employ environmental monitoring and warning systems.* International organizations have already established global environmental monitoring and warning systems, notably the U.N. Environment Programme's Global Environmental Monitoring System (GEMS).

- *Provide improved climate data for direct use.* The newly established Climate Data Programme and Climate Applications Programme, part of the WMO's World Climate Programme, should improve the availability and application of climate data for planning and operations. There are many countries that lack the expertise or the computers needed to make use of our knowledge of climate and its influence on human activities.

- *Inform and educate the public.* Dissemination of the latest results of climate studies should raise the general level of public awareness about the carbon dioxide/climate problem. This will lead, one can hope, to better choices by political leaders and a greater public acceptance of long term measures to cope with climatic variations and change.

- *Transfer appropriate technology.* The transfer of technology to developing countries has been taking place for a long time, but it has not always been appropriate. Technology tailored to developing countries' needs will help in agriculture, water resources, the development of export products, and land use.

Clearly, nations need to take vigorous initiatives to cope with our changing environment. Whether societies will have the resources needed to adapt to climatic changes will be determined by several indices, most of them economic: gross national product (GNP), an indicator of the economic resources available to build new facilities or move people; ratio of investment to GNP (or gross rate of investment), an indicator of the rate of turnover of new facilities and capital stock (a faster turnover implies more flexibility); the flexibility and diversity of the capital stock, which, though it may increase costs and lower output somewhat, offers insurance against changing conditions; and the ability to foresee changing conditions and adapt to them quickly, which comes with public information and education.

## International Institutions and Legal Mechanisms

### History of organizations for environmental cooperation

Formal recognition of the need for international collection and exchanges of meteorological and oceanographic observations occurred in 1873 with the establishment of the International Meteorological Organization (IMO). In 1951 the IMO became the WMO, one of the United Nations' specialized intergovernmental agencies; it now has its headquarters in Geneva, Switzerland.

Until recently the WMO devoted most of its effort to improving weather forecasting and exchanging worldwide meteorological observations twice a day through the World Weather Watch (WWW) system. However, more attention has been paid to climate in the past few years. In February, 1979, the WMO held the first World Climate Conference in Geneva to approve a draft proposal for a new World Climate Programme. This Programme was implemented at the beginning of 1980.

There are four components of the World Climate Programme: the *Climate Data Programme*, devoted primarily to helping developing countries organize and use their climate data; the *Climate Applications Programme*, also primarily aimed at helping developing countries make better use of our knowledge of climate; the *Climate Research Programme*, a continuation of the Global Atmospheric Research Programme (GARP) and devoted to obtaining a better understanding of the physical basis for climate and climate change (jointly sponsored by the WMO and the International Council of Scientific Unions); and the *Climate Impact Studies Programme*, whose objectives are, to a large extent, the subject of this report. The U.N. Environment Programme (UNEP) has assumed the responsibility for this last program.

During the 1970s there was a growing concern for the environment and its finite natural resources. Following the U.N. Conference on the Human Environment in Stockholm in June, 1972, UNEP was established, with headquarters in Nairobi, Kenya. Its charter includes dissemination of "information on major environmental problems and the efforts being made to respond to them, in order to identify gaps, set objectives, and establish priorities." To meet these goals, one step UNEP has taken was organizing the Global Environmental Monitoring System (GEMS). Among GEMS' functions is "assessing global atmospheric pollution and its impact on climate."

The International Council of Scientific Unions (ICSU), a non-governmental body, founded the Scientific Committee on Problems of the Environment (SCOPE) in 1969. This has expanded the opportunity for international collaboration. One of SCOPE's activities is a long term study of biogeochemical cycles of carbon, nitrogen, phosphorous, and sulfur which would be affected by climate change.

Another organization conducting research on global problems is the International Institute for Applied Systems Analysis (IIASA), located in Laxenburg, Austria. Presently IIASA's membership consists of 17 national scientific academies, and its research has included studies of world energy and food problems and their climatic implications.

There are also several regional associations of nations that are becoming more active in this field. The Council of European Communities, for example, has adopted a European Climate Programme similar to the U.S. National Climate Program.

## International legal mechanisms

We should not expect too much of international law when it comes to resolving cases that deal with injuries or damages caused by carbon dioxide–induced climate change. Ultimately, countries are free to comply with or ignore international law. In any case, there is currently no mechanism by which to set carbon dioxide standards and establish universally applied control measures, nor a policing body to enforce the so-called "global right to a clean atmosphere."

It would make sense, however, to encourage new international mechanisms that could, among other things: examine the likely effects of a carbon dioxide–induced warming on national and international activities; recommend to governments, as far as practical, measures to deter "excessive" use of fossil fuel or large scale deforestation; and exchange information on climate change and its impacts. The Climate Impact Studies Programme may be in a position to fulfill some of these functions.

There are some existing international mechanisms that could become applicable to carbon dioxide related issues in the next few decades. They include:

- *International agreements.* The Organization for Economic Cooperation and Development (OECD) Environmental Committee has given some attention to atmospheric carbon dioxide. In 1979, the Council on Coal and the Environment specifically recommended that: "Member countries, in the light of appropriate research results, seek to define acceptable fuel qualities, emissions levels or ambient media qualities, as appropriate, for carbon dioxide."

  In 1979, the European Commission for Europe signed a "Convention on Transboundary Air Pollution." The 34 member states, including the U.S. and Canada, pledged "to limit, and, as far as possible, gradually reduce and prevent air pollution."

  There are other types of treaties and conventions being negotiated that apply principles of international law to established areas of transnational significance, such as marine pollution, nuclear weapons tests, exploitation of the Antarctic, and the use of outer space. Nations engaging in these agreements have taken preliminary steps toward clarifying the procedures through which regulations can be implemented.

  There seems to be a growing acceptance of regional organizations such as the European Economic Community, the OECD, the Council for Mutual Economic Aid, the Association of Southeast Asian Nations, and the Latin America Free Trade Association, among others. These groups are set up to deal with specific supranational problems. They could be valuable in implementing carbon dioxide control strategies, and in compensating member countries for damages resulting from climate change.

- *International commissions.* The findings and recommendations of international commissions such as "conciliation commissions," "arbitral tribunals," and "commissions of inquiry" can sometimes influence international behavior. For carbon dioxide problems such commissions may be useful ad hoc devices to either arbitrate disputes or gather expert opinions on controversial legal, political, and scientific issues.

- *International conferences.* Conducting international negotiations through special conferences is becoming an accepted practice among countries. The United Nations has encouraged this by convening such meetings as the Conferences on the Environment, the Law of the Sea, the Law of Treaties, and Science and Technology for Development.

The value of recommendations made at international conferences is that they tend to call attention to matters that *should* be dealt with by the member states. To date, the World Climate Conference has been the largest international conference to investigate the impacts of climatic change.

We have only dealt with a few of the possible international legal mechanisms for handling the political and economic consequences of a global carbon dioxide–induced climatic change. Special mention should also be made of diplomatic negotiations, the Permanent Court of Arbitration, and the International Court of Justice. Each of these may be used to resolve possible carbon dioxide related damage and compensation disputes. It seems unlikely, however, that any of them can be effective in achieving worldwide action to reduce fossil fuel use.

## Ethical Considerations

Ethical issues that arise from carbon dioxide–induced climate changes may influence future national and international actions. Assessing "blame" for carbon dioxide emissions is one such issue.

We believe that the cumulative amount of carbon dioxide over the years should be considered instead of annual emissions, or those projected for some future date. Developing countries have been identified as the future heavy users of fossil fuels. But it is more likely that the developed countries and their profligate use of energy will account for most of the atmospheric carbon dioxide buildup in this century and the first part of the next century. Thus, developing countries cannot be held reponsible for the cumulative amounts of carbon dioxide pollution.

The precise costs and benefits of a global warming may be difficult if not impossible to assess quantitatively. Hence, it may be more practical to determine the proportional indemnity to be charged countries; these countries would then pay for carbon dioxide control measures. Establishing and drawing on environmental damage funds might be one way to compensate nations adversely affected by carbon dioxide–induced impacts.

International technology and resource transfers to developing countries and assistance in applying climatological information at local levels are also measures that might be encouraged. Indeed, the latter is one of the objectives of the World Climate Programme.

Other ethical issues concern the rights to food and a clean atmosphere. Of course, these rights are contingent on national and international obligations; in the case of carbon dioxide–induced climate shifts that result in decreased food production or environmental damages, the exercise of rights hinges on finding ways to justify and compensate claims.

A different set of ethical issues arises when considering the obligations of the present generation to protect the welfare of future generations. Economists as well as the public tend to "discount the future," as already pointed out. There is no clear answer to the question of how much we should sacrifice now for the long term benefits of society. Ethical considerations doubtless influence our decisions. An example of this is the "environmental ethic" that has led to preserving wilderness areas for future generations, even when it means losing an economic asset for today's generation.

There are some long term strategies to mitigate the future impacts of climatic change, some of which will involve costs and sacrifices now if they are implemented. We have emphasized that these strategies can provide some short term benefits as well. Hence such decisions, motivated by altruistic considerations, can also serve our immediate self interest.

## Conclusion

We would like to reiterate a few of the more important points that emerge regarding societal impacts of a carbon dioxide–induced climatic change.

While we may never be able to predict future climatic change and how societies will respond to it, we can clarify the relative merits of alternative long term policies or strategies. We believe that the most useful strategies are those that can mitigate the adverse impacts of the changes and make specific activities — such as agriculture and human settlement — less vulnerable to climatic impacts from whatever cause.

Having made an initial (and by no means exhaustive) examination of the various strategies, we can see that each one will also help cope with short term weather and climate variability — devastating events such as droughts, floods, heat waves, and cold spells that cause hardship every year. Some strategies will also help alleviate environmental problems such as the loss of arable soil and tropical forests; international and national measures to preserve these precious natural assets are long overdue. Perhaps the stimulus of an impending climate change will help to spur such actions.

Climatic impact studies will help to estimate the effects of climatic changes, which should enable us to better plan agricultural production, land use, and human settlements, and to develop water resources and marketing strategies. However, new and improved methodologies of climate impact assessment are needed as well as more scientists interested in working on impact studies.

Thus far, we have emphasized two areas of such studies. First is the development of climate scenarios. While not predictions of the future climate on a warmer Earth, scenarios are descriptions of the possible regional and seasonal patterns of temperature, precipitation, soil moisture, and sea level. More detailed scenarios on possible future climatic shifts are badly needed by planners and policy makers.

Second is the development of economic methodologies. These should be able to analyze the effects of climatic change in quantitative terms. But conventional cost/benefit models are still not well adapted to such analyses. Further interdisciplinary studies will provide an opportunity to improve the methodology of climatic impact assessment.

Apart from the research needed to improve our ability to carry out impact studies, it is imperative that we implement international programs to cope with carbon dioxide–induced changes. Some international mechanisms already exist that might help us deal with this unprecedented set of global problems. All of them should be explored and their use encouraged. Most importantly, nations should be made aware of the problem of climatic change and of the strategies that could mitigate its effects.

For some countries the change may be favorable, while for others it may be adverse. But we must emphasize that the prospect of a global climatic change is just one of a number of global environmental and societal problems. In the first half of the next century the world could well have twice as many people, consume three times as much food, and burn four times as much energy. Thus, impacts of climatic change must be superimposed on this backdrop. Our future problems will be serious even without a shifting climate.

# I. INTRODUCTION

## 1. Climatic Change in Perspective

A new factor has recently been introduced into the delicate balance of forces that determine the Earth's climate — *mankind*.

It is general knowledge that human activities are very likely to cause a change in the global climate in the decades ahead, provided we continue to depend on fossil fuels (coal, oil, and natural gas) as our main energy source. There have been many studies of this matter, and few climatologists (if any) still doubt that the Earth is probably due for a general warming. The timing of this event is uncertain, but a reasonable "best guess" is that 20 years from now the average global temperature will be as warm or warmer than at any time in the past thousand years and it will still be rising. Such a temperature change will surely be accompanied by shifts of rainfall patterns and an altered distribution of snow and ice.

While there are admittedly a number of uncertainties in this forecast of future climate change, it is already becoming a matter of worldwide concern. This concern has led to a new set of questions regarding the impact such a climate change will have on human activities that are sensitive to climate — as most of them are — and on the very structure of societies. It is no longer enough to speak of the future climate in terms of temperature and rainfall. *We must define it in human terms.*

This report attempts to examine climatic change in light of human affairs. It will briefly describe what is presently known about the physical factors that determine climate, including in particular the effect of increasing atmospheric carbon dioxide from burning fossil fuels. This will lay the groundwork for the body of this report, which deals with activities that are potentially sensitive to climatic change, and the various strategies we could use at the local, national, and international levels to adapt to the change, mitigate its adverse impacts, or perhaps even avert the change.

Our purpose in preparing this report is not so much to provide answers as to clarify *what needs to be done to get the answers.* It is, in a sense, a general blueprint for a research program that can develop increasingly reliable tools for assessing alternative long term plans for energy production and use, food, forestry, water resources, and land use.

In all these areas changing climate must figure prominently, as it should in a number of other pressing international environmental problems. The loss of arable topsoil, spread of deserts, acid rain, and deforestation in the tropics are all affected by the climate.

It follows that any study of climatic impacts must be highly interdisciplinary; it must challenge experts in climatology, oceanography, agronomy, political science, economics, geography, and engineering, to name a few. These experts must learn each others' languages and how to work together. This is not easy in our current academic establishment which usually encourages specialization as the best way to get ahead. But it is increasingly clear that most of society's pressing problems require an interdisciplinary approach (DOE, 1979a; 1979b).

Our intended audience for this report includes national and international political leaders who must make policy decisions in light of the best knowledge available, the research administrators and scientists who must supply this knowledge, and the members of an informed citizenry who will shape public opinion. In particular, this report should give some guidance to those who are motivated to study these pressing climate related problems at the interfaces between the geophysical, biological, and social sciences.

## 2. Scope of the Problem and the Cascade of Uncertainty

It has been necessary in this report to structure the immensely complex subject of climatic impact studies in terms of a sequence or hierarchy of problems, even though such a structuring may appear arbitrary in some respects. The order chosen is imposed by the cascade of cause–and–effect that starts with burning fossil fuels (and possibly by deforestation as well) and leads more or less inexorably to a complex set of societal impacts. This cascade of interactions can be summarized in terms of a series of problems to be studied:

a. For a given scenario of fossil fuel use, determine the future levels of carbon dioxide concentration in the atmosphere.
b. For a given scenario of carbon dioxide concentration, determine the resulting climatic change in terms of regional and seasonal patterns of temperatures, precipitation, and soil moisture, among other variables.
c. For a given scenario of polar region climatic change, determine

24

what will happen to the volume of the major ice sheets and the subsequent effect on sea level.

d. For a given scenario of regional and seasonal climatic change, determine the effects on specific activities such as agriculture, land use, water resources, industry, transportation, and energy requirements on a country–by–country or region–by–region basis.

e. For a given scenario of specific socioeconomic effects, determine the probable or desirable responses of societies.

f. Along with the preceding set of considerations, determine the influences on earlier aspects of the problem, or "feedbacks", resulting from implementing alternative strategies to mitigate the impacts or, perhaps, to avert the climatic change.

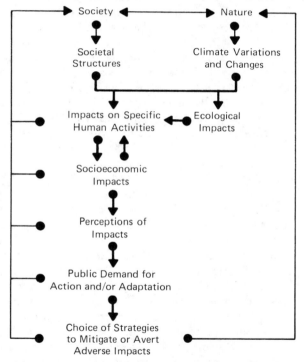

**Figure I.1** **The interconnected components that are involved in climate impact studies. Note that society and nature combine to influence societal structures; therefore climatic changes and variation by themselves do not determine climatic impacts (Adapted from Kates, 1979).**

25

This cascade of cause–and–effect closes back on itself in the last step; the resulting impacts will therefore be influenced by the actions of people and their institutions. These important feedback loops are illustrated in Figure I.1.

The research needed to take steps a, b, and c will be outlined in Chapter II. The research needed for steps d, e, and f will be the subject of chapters III and IV.

While each area of study in the hierarchy of problems depends to a certain extent on outputs of the earlier studies in the sequence, this definitely does not mean that one must await those outputs before proceeding to the next step. As one economist put it, "We cannot stand around waiting for the climatologists to finish their homework; we must start now thinking about possible mitigating strategies."

It is important to realize that the uncertainties in our understanding of climatic impacts will most likely increase as we move down the cascade of cause–and–effect from predictions of fossil fuel use, to development of climate scenarios, to foreseeing socioeconomic implications. That is to say, uncertainty is likely to increase as we study the more indirect or secondary implications of climatic change, and as we move deeper into the possible development of international strategies to manage the "global commons." This may be thought of as a "cascade of uncertainty," shown schematically in Figure I.2. Here food and energy considerations are displayed, but the same uncertainties probably also apply to such activities as management of water resources, transportation, and land use, to name a few.

The following set of questions must now be asked: If there are so many uncertainties in our understanding of climatic impacts, can we make any useful predictions of their implications? Are there ways to build resilience (that is, decrease our vulnerability) to climatic changes, whether carbon dioxide–induced or natural? Will decision makers be willing to rely on the results of scientific inquiry? What incentives and deterrents exist for taking policy action on the carbon dioxide/climatic issue? What is the long term purpose of the research effort?

While there are no very clear answers to this set of questions, the following considerations may help to put the carbon dioxide/climatic impact research program into better perspective. First, no prediction of the future can be made until the climatic change and its geophysical implications can be described in more detail and with more assurance than can be done now. For example, we need to know what to expect in terms of regional and seasonal changes of rainfall and temperature. Second, there appear to be a great many techniques already at hand to assess the effects of a given climatic change on certain specific human

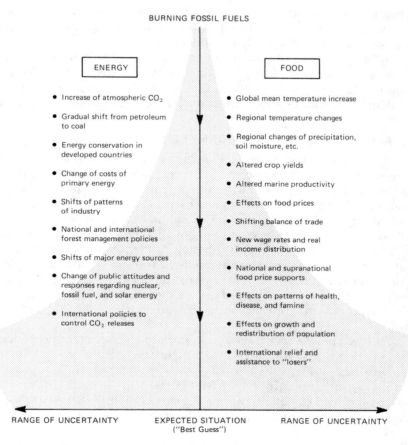

BURNING FOSSIL FUELS

| ENERGY | FOOD |
|---|---|

ENERGY

- Increase of atmospheric $CO_2$
- Gradual shift from petroleum to coal
- Energy conservation in developed countries
- Change of costs of primary energy
- Shifts of patterns of industry
- National and international forest management policies
- Shifts of major energy sources
- Change of public attitudes and responses regarding nuclear, fossil fuel, and solar energy
- International policies to control $CO_2$ releases

FOOD

- Global mean temperature increase
- Regional temperature changes
- Regional changes of precipitation, soil moisture, etc.
- Altered crop yields
- Altered marine productivity
- Effects on food prices
- Shifting balance of trade
- New wage rates and real income distribution
- National and supranational food price supports
- Effects on patterns of health, disease, and famine
- Effects on growth and redistribution of population
- International relief and assistance to "losers"

◄———— RANGE OF UNCERTAINTY        EXPECTED SITUATION        RANGE OF UNCERTAINTY ————►
                                        ("Best Guess")

**Figure I.2**  **A schematic representation of the range of uncertainty regarding future impacts from climatic change. As the more secondary impacts (such as shifts of patterns of industry or government interventions) come into play, there is more uncertainty about the outcome. While the economic sectors of energy and food are used as examples, the same would apply to other sectors such as water resources.**

activities, such as crop models that predict how the growth of a particular kind of plant will be affected by the weather. These techniques need to be further developed and applied to a wider variety of activities, but the point is that many of them are available. Third, the public and decision makers need to be made aware of the alternatives open to them. Even though we probably cannot predict mankind's long term future behavior, impact studies can provide the information needed to

27

comprehend the implications of choosing alternative strategies. Decisions will have to be made, and they should be made in light of our best perceptions of the likely consequences.

In Figure I.1 the point was made that "perceptions of impacts" must precede any "choice of response" or decision. Providing clearer and responsible perceptions of future climatic impacts, then, can be considered one of the major long term goals of this program of research.

## 3. Actions Spurred by Environmental Change

It will be shown in more detail later in this report how actions taken to alleviate immediate environmental threats are also likely to increase a country or region's ability to withstand a change of climate, whether it is an anomaly of the weather or a long term trend in the climate. Improving water storage and irrigation systems is a good example of a measure that will increase the resilience of a region, in this case to the stress of droughts. Another example of building resilience is reforesting areas that have been cleared. The regrowth of trees will provide the next generation with lumber and firewood, control erosion of topsoil, and also help take some of the added carbon dioxide out of the atmosphere. (Photosynthesis in growing trees converts carbon dioxide to plant tissue.)

Thus we have a recurrent and important theme: identify the long term strategies that will increase each country's resilience to climatic change. These strategies will usually make sense for several reasons and should be adopted in any case. Perhaps the issue of carbon dioxide-induced climatic change will serve as stimulus to employ these strategies sooner. Many of them are long overdue.

# REFERENCES

DOE, 1979a: *Workshop on the Global Effects of Carbon Dioxide from Fossil Fuels.* W. P. Elliott and L. Machta (eds.), Miami Beach, Fla., 7-11, March, U.S. Dept. of Energy, Washington, D.C. (CONF-770385, UC-11).

DOE, 1979b: *Workshop on Environmental and Societal Consequences of a Possible CO$_2$-Induced Climate Change.* Annapolis, Md., 2-6 April, U.S. Dept. of Energy, Washington, D.C.

Kates, R.W., 1979: *Improving the science of impact study.* Proposal to ICSU Scientific Committee on Problems of the Environment (SCOPE), Paris, November.

# II. CARBON DIOXIDE AND CLIMATIC CHANGE

## 1. Introduction to Climate Research

In the previous chapter we defined climatic impact studies as dealing with a sequence or hierarchy of problem areas, beginning with research on the natural system. What is often referred to as simply "climate research" is an essential element in the hierarchy of problems that we discuss in this report.

Climate research is the subject of this chapter, and subsequent chapters will treat the socioeconomic and political implications of climatic change. It is difficult to study these implications without some notion of the potential climatic changes in store, and a feel for the gaps in our current knowledge. Climatologists, therefore, are obligated to share this information with their colleagues in the social sciences.

We will consider three main areas of climate research:

- *The physical changes that human activities can bring about* in some of the components of the climate system, shown in Figure II.1. We will emphasize the increase in fossil fuel use and atmospheric carbon dioxide and also explore how we

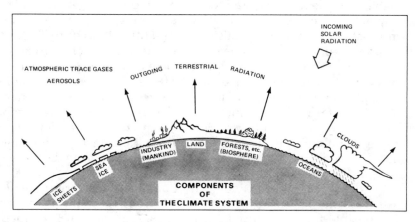

**Figure II.1. These components of the Earth's climate system interact with each other, together determining the climate (Kellogg, 1979).**

may be altering the global ecological system, especially the forests of the world.

- *The response of the climate system to those induced changes,* with emphasis on atmospheric carbon dioxide. A special topic here is the response of the polar regions, with their masses of ice and snow, to a global warming.

- *The integration of our knowledge of future influences* of human activities using climate scenarios. These scenarios must be drawn from several sources, including theoretical models of the climate system and the history of past climates. They must be as detailed as possible, presenting the changes of temperature, rainfall, and soil moisture as a function of season for each region of the world. Climatologists cannot yet presume to draw up such scenarios in the form of actual predictions of the future climate, but they can begin to describe the range of climate possiblities.

## 2. Influences of Human Activities on the Climate System

### 2.1 "Levers" in the climate system

At the turn of this century scientists suggested that the carbon dioxide added to the atmosphere from burning fossil fuels could influence the global climate (Chamberlain, 1899; Arrhenius, 1903). Nevertheless, a decade ago the prevailing attitude was that the global climate system (Figure II.1) is probably too enormous and too stable — some have referred to it as "very robust" — to respond to anything we could do to it. However, a landmark review by an international group of scientists in 1971 (SMIC, 1971) dispelled that notion. And, the more we learn about the atmospheric processes involved, the more convinced we become that there are a variety of ways by which we can change the climate, especially if we continue to exploit energy, land, and living resources at an increasing rate. We may refer to these influences as "levers" in the climate system that we can reach and by which we can control the climate — though that control is usually inadvertent (Kellogg and Schneider, 1974). In order to condense the discussion of the many levers, we will summarize them in Table II.1.

Adding carbon dioxide turns out to be the largest single anthropogenic change that may influence climate in the foreseeable future (SMIC, 1971; NAS, 1977; IIASA, 1978; Kellogg, 1978; 1979); it will be treated in Section 2.2. The addition of other

**Table II.1. Human activities influencing climate (Kellogg, 1979).**

| Activity | Climatic effect | Scale and importance of the effect |
|---|---|---|
| Release of carbon dioxide by burning fossil fuels | Increases the atmospheric absorption and emission of terrestrial infrared radiation (greenhouse effect) resulting in warming of lower atmosphere and cooling of the stratosphere | Global; potentially a major influence on climate |
| Release of chlorofluoromethanes, nitrous oxide, carbon tetrachloride, carbon disulfide, etc. | Same effect as that of carbon dioxide since these, too, are infrared-absorbing and chemically stable trace gases | Global; potentially significant |
| Release of particles (aerosols) from industry and slash-and-burn practices | These sunlight-absorbing particles probably decrease albedo over land, causing a warming; they also change stability of lower atmosphere | Regional, since aerosols have an average lifetime of only a few days; stability increase may suppress convective rainfall |
| Release of heat (thermal pollution) | Warms the lower atmosphere directly | Locally important now; will become significant regionally; could modify large-scale circulation |
| Release of aerosols that act as condensation and freezing nuclei | Influences growth of cloud droplets and ice crystals; may affect precipitation in either direction | Local or (at most) regional influence on precipitation |
| Upward transport of chlorofluoromethanes and nitrous oxide into the stratosphere | Photochemical reaction of their dissociation products reduces stratospheric ozone | Global; probably small influences on climate; allows more solar ultraviolet radiation to reach the surface |
| Patterns of land use, e.g. urbanization, agriculture, overgrazing, deforestation, etc. | Changes surface albedo and evapotranspiration | Regional; global importance speculative |
| Release of radioactive Krypton-85 from nuclear reactors and fuel reprocessing plants | Increases conductivity of lower atmosphere, with implications for electric field and precipitation from convective clouds | Global; importance of influence is highly speculative |

infrared–absorbing gases to the atmosphere may add significantly to the carbon dioxide–induced warming and will also be discussed below.

The release of heat worldwide from large urban–industrial complexes and power parks deserves special mention because it is often referred to as a potentially important factor. But in order to be important globally, this "thermal pollution" must either add appreciably to the solar heat being absorbed at the Earth's surface, or it must somehow change the large scale atmospheric circulation patterns. Currently, the worldwide total of human generated heat release is about 10TW**. This compares to $8 \times 10^4$ TW of heat from the Sun that is absorbed at the surface of the Earth. The difference is almost a factor of 10,000; our thermal pollution would have to be increased 100 times to account for even a 1°C change of average surface temperatures. Such a large increase in worldwide power consumption would almost surely not occur before 2100, if ever (Kahn et al., 1976; Kellogg, 1978). In any case, before 2100 a warming from carbon dioxide would probably prevail.

As for altering the large scale circulation patterns with thermal pollution, inordinate amounts of heat would have to be released. At least two independent experiments with state–of–the–art climate models have been performed, in which enormous power parks or urban–industrial complexes were introduced as heat sources at the surface (Llewellyn and Washington, 1977; Williams et al., 1979). The models showed that, in order to even slightly alter the circulation patterns, 150 to 300 TW of thermal power would have to be introduced. This is more than 15 times the total worldwide power generated now. Thus, while the release of anthropogenic heat can affect the local environment now (cities are usually warmer than the surrounding countryside, a phenomenon called the "urban heat island effect"), it appears to be fairly insignificant on a global scale in the foreseeable future.

## 2.2 Buildup of atmospheric carbon dioxide

In order to deal with increased carbon dioxide we need to understand how it is added to and removed from the atmosphere — that is, the "carbon cycle". The Scientific Committee on Problems of the Environment (SCOPE, 1979), has published a detailed account of this process. Their main conclusions are summarized in the report of an ad hoc Study Group of the National Academy of Sciences (NAS)

---

**One terrawatt (TW) equals $10^{12}$ watts.

Climate Research Board, which met at Woods Hole in July, 1979 (NAS, 1979). We will only briefly review the subject here, drawing in part from these two sources, and provide more complete information on past and future use of fossil fuel in Appendix A.

Just before the Industrial Revolution, the natural sources and sinks of carbon dioxide must have been in near–equilibrium. Undoubtedly there have been large changes in carbon dioxide concentration during the Earth's geological history. In fact there have been changes of a factor of two in just the past 20,000 years (Berner et al., 1980; Delmas et al., 1980). One hundred years ago the concentration of carbon dioxide was probably between 270 and 290 parts per million by volume (ppmv). But at that time there was a new source introduced. Mankind began taking carbon locked in the Earth's crust in the form of coal, petroleum, and natural gas and burning it, thereby producing carbon dioxide. Since the turn of the century the rate of carbon dioxide increase from burning fossil fuels has been about 4.3 percent per year, a steady rise that slackened only during the two world wars and the 1930s depression (Rotty, 1979; Appendix A). Carbon dioxide concentration is now almost 336 ppmv, a 17 percent increase over the pre–Industrial Revolution value. This long term increase is shown in Figure II.2.

The United Nations has •calculated how much fossil fuel has been used worldwide. These figures make it possible to compare the cumulative amount of carbon dioxide produced with the amount that has remained in the atmosphere. It appears that about 55 percent is still airborne. Generally, it has been assumed that the rest was taken up by the oceans, or possibly by the living biota — that is, primarily the forests of the world. We will first discuss what part the forests play.

Perceptions of the biosphere's role have altered in the past few years. Originally, the biota were assumed to take up a fraction of the new carbon dioxide emissions, since plants grow faster when their concentration is increased (SMIC, 1971; Bacastow and Keeling, 1973; Machta, 1973). But then some scientists pointed out that the forests of the world, most of which are in the tropics, may have been cut down at a rate much faster than their regrowth. Therefore, the living biomass could have been an additional source rather than a sink for the carbon dioxide. According to one study (Sommer, 1976) sponsored by the Food and Agriculture Organization (FAO), the tropical forests of the world may have been shrinking at a rate of more than 1 percent per year. If true, this could account for a source roughly equal to burning fossil fuels (Woodwell et al., 1978).

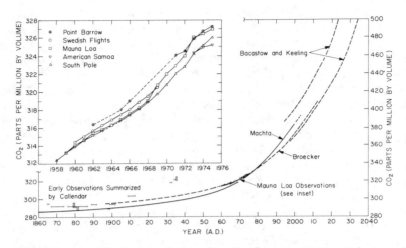

**Figure II.2.** **The long term rise in atmospheric carbon dioxide content starting at the time of the Industrial Revolution and continuing into the next century. The early data were critically reviewed by Callendar (1958) and subsequently reevaluated by Barrett (1975). The current series of observations for Mauna Loa are those reported by Keeling et al. (1976b) and C.D. Keeling (private communication), for South Pole by Keeling et al. (1976a) and C.D. Keeling (private communication), for American Samoa and Point Barrow by NOAA (1975) and T. Harris (private communication), and for the Swedish aircraft observations by Bolin and Bischof (1970). The model calculations predicting future carbon dioxide increases by Machta (1973), Broecker (1975), and Bacastow and Keeling (1973) all take account of the uptake of anthropogenic carbon dioxide by oceans and the biosphere (but in somewhat different ways), and assume a nearly exponential increase in the rate of burning of fossil fuels (notably coal) in the next half century or more. It is expected that, in this time period, about half of the new carbon dioxide released will remain in the atmosphere.**

However, this estimate appears to be very uncertain; it was based on incomplete data concerning tropical deforestation referring to only 18 percent of the total forest area, which is an inadequate sample. Furthermore it now appears that Woodwell et al., (1978) may have overestimated the mass of the tropical forests by almost a factor of two (Kerr, 1980). Also, Seiler and Crutzen (1980) have shown that the wood converted to charcoal may be a sink that had been overlooked, since charcoal decomposes extremely slowly.

Other evidence, based on how fast the oceans can absorb carbon dioxide and models of the carbon cycle, now points to a biomass contribution of from 0 to 40 percent of the current yearly fossil fuel contribution (Björkstrom, 1979a; Broecker et al., 1979; Seiler and Crutzen, 1980). But this question is far from resolved.

36

Whether or not deforestation is a large source of carbon dioxide makes some difference in near term estimates of its future atmospheric concentration, but as the fossil fuel consumption rate goes up (if it does) this difference becomes relatively less and less important (Zimen et al., 1977).

There are at least two other possible sources of carbon dioxide that humans can influence indirectly. Organic matter in soils is one. When we plow or otherwise disturb soil, organic compounds are oxidized and released into the air. But estimates of the carbon dioxide contribution from this source are even more uncertain than estimates for the forest source (TIE, 1980).

There is also the long term possibility that a prolonged warming at high latitudes in the Northern Hemisphere would cause the permafrost to retreat. This would dry out the upper layers of the deep beds of organic matter (peat and tundra) and allow them to oxidize. It is a "positive feedback" or amplification factor, since the extra carbon dioxide would add to the warming, but presumably it would operate quite slowly (see Section III.4).

As mentioned earlier, the oceans have been able to take up about 45 percent of the accumulated carbon dioxide — this figure assumes there were no sources other than fossil fuels. But if deforestation has indeed added another 40 percent, the oceans must have taken up the equivalent of over 80 percent of the fossil fuel contribution. The rate at which carbon dioxide can be absorbed at the ocean surface and mixed downward is somewhat uncertain, but there are studies of the downward transport (or diffusion) of carbon–14 and tritium from the atomic tests of the early 1960s. These reports indicate that the oceans are apparently incapable of accepting as much as 80 percent of added atmospheric carbon dioxide (Broecker et al., 1979; Stuiver, 1978).

In order to predict the future level of carbon dioxide in the atmosphere, we need to better understand the way in which the upper mixed layer of the oceans exchanges water with the more stable layers below it — the region of the thermocline (where temperature decreases with increasing depth) and the region below that. A number of theoretical models have been developed to predict the oceans' ability to take up carbon dioxide over the long term (e.g., Keeling and Bacastow 1977; Revelle and Munk, 1977; Siegenthaler and Oeschger, 1978; Björkstrom, 1979b). They all involve a slow exchange between the upper mixed layer and the deep waters, which is what prevents the oceans from absorbing carbon dioxide as fast as it is produced. If carbon dioxide increases exponentially, the fraction taken up by the oceans theoretically becomes less and this increases the airborne fraction. (In Figure II.2 the extrapolation into the next century involved various assumptions about the rate at which oceans and biota would take up the added carbon dioxide.)

The oceans can eventually absorb a very large increase of carbon dioxide as the deep waters are gradually exchanged with the upper layers. However, it is estimated that the time for such an exchange to occur is more than 500 years. This means that on the time scale of human affairs the atmospheric carbon dioxide increase that we have already witnessed will persist, even if we were to stop emitting it tomorrow.

## 3.   Carbon Dioxide and Climatic Change

The previous section described the way in which atmospheric carbon dioxide has been increasing, and the problems involved in predicting its future change. While we do not fully understand the carbon cycle, we do know without a doubt that carbon dioxide is indeed increasing and will continue to do so as long as we burn fossil fuels (see Figure II.2).

The next set of questions we must ask relates to the effect of the added carbon dioxide on the climate. This gas absorbs the infrared radiation coming from the Earth's surface and reradiates a part of it back down, thereby warming the planet. This is referred to as the "greenhouse effect." The radiative effects of carbon dioxide are well understood, and if this were the only factor involved we could accurately predict the change in atmospheric heat balance for, say, a doubling of carbon dioxide. However, as will be shown, there are many other factors, or "feedback mechanisms," that must also be taken into account.

Furthermore, there are other infrared–absorbing trace gases being added to the atmosphere by humans, such as chlorofluoromethanes, methane, carbon monoxide, nitrous oxide, and ozone. These could increase the greenhouse warming by as much as another 50 percent above the warming from carbon dioxide alone (Flohn, 1979; Hameed et al., 1980; Ramanathan, 1980).

It is well recognized that the Sun warms the equator more than the poles. This is because the Earth's surface at the equator lies more perpendicular to the Sun's rays whereas the poles receive only glancing rays. Hot air from the equator rises and moves poleward while the cooler polar air sinks and flows toward the equator. This air movement is the driving force for the atmospheric and oceanic circulations, and it transports heat and water vapor from the equator to the poles — it is, in fact, a gigantic heat engine. Thus, any change in the distribution of heating, as would occur as a result of an intensified greenhouse effect, will change the circulation patterns of the atmosphere and oceans in a complex way. These patterns determine distributions of temperature, cloudiness, precipitation, and ice coverage — indeed, they are the key to the Earth's weather and climate.

In the following discussion, climate will be considered in its broadest sense, including the state of the ice and snow masses of the polar regions, called the "cryosphere." As will be shown, the cryosphere is an integral part of the system that determines climate (see Figure II.1). Alterations in polar climate will have an influence on climate elsewhere, especially at high latitudes. Furthermore, the ice sheets of Greenland and the Antarctic contain so much water that any change in their volume will affect sea level, with serious implications for society: melting and reduction of the ice sheets could increase sea levels which would then flood coastal areas.

### 3.1. Experiments with climate models

There are, of course, a great many factors at work in the system that ultimately controls climate. The challenge faced by the climate modeler is to take all of the important ones into account. Using computer generated simulations of the atmosphere, the modeler seeks to develop enough insight into the system to be able to specify how the atmosphere and oceans will respond to a given increase in carbon dioxide.

Climate models have reached a new level of sophistication in recent years, but how well do they actually simulate the behavior of the climate system? And more importantly, can they tell us about the climatic changes in store for the world — such as the alterations in *regional* and *seasonal* temperatures, precipitation, and soil moisture — with the accuracy and detail needed for impact studies and long range planning?

These questions have been asked many times, most recently by the National Academy of Sciences ad hoc Study Group meeting at Woods Hole, Massachusetts (NAS, 1979) and by the ad hoc Study Group on Climatic Effects of Increased Carbon Dioxide of the World Meteorological Organization (WMO) Commission on Atmospheric Science meeting in Boulder, Colorado (WMO, 1979b), which we mentioned earlier. Both of these working groups critically assessed the results of experiments with a variety of climate models, and considered whether there were any identifiable deficiencies in the models that would cause them to behave very differently from the "real thing."

Before summarizing these findings we should point out the following: We can gain a great deal of insight from studies of past climatic changes (as we will discuss in more detail later), and from some relatively simple one and two-dimensional models of the atmosphere that permit us to study specific relationships. But numerical models are the primary tools to which we must ultimately turn. They include the atmosphere, oceans, land, vegetation, and snow and ice in as much physical and spatial detail as computer time and human ingenuity will permit. There has never been a climatic situation exactly like the one we envision from increasing carbon dioxide concentrations. Therefore we must arm ourselves with "first principle" information such as that contained in numerical models, rather than rely too heavily on analogies from the past.

The climate models in question are dissimilar in many respects, but most of them include an atmosphere in which the motions, heat exchanges, and hydrologic cycle are included explicitly. The processes at the surface of the land, ocean, or ice cover and in the boundary layer of the lower atmosphere are considered in varying degrees of detail. In fact, in some models this information reproduces a three-dimensional atmosphere that appears to simulate the present varying weather and average climate quite well, including the changing seasons. Such time-dependent three-dimensional atmospheric models are referred to as "general circulation models," or GCMs.

However, a GCM by itself does not constitute a climate model, since the oceans are excluded. In some respects the oceans are even more important in determining the climate than the atmosphere. Apparently the oceans transfer nearly as much heat from equator to pole at middle latitudes as does the atmosphere, are the source of most of the atmospheric water vapor, and regulate the surface temperature of four-fifths of the globe. Thus, a complete climate model must include the oceans in some way. However, oceans seem to be harder to model than the atmosphere. Hence, the climate models used so far in experiments to determine the response to increased carbon dioxide include oceans that are highly simplified (see Appendix B). One approach has been to let the simulated ocean be an infinite source of water vapor, but with no heat capacity and no circulation, very much like an enormous swamp. Another approach has been to consider just the upper mixed layer of the ocean, the part some 70 meters deep that responds to seasonal changes of temperature. Again, circulation and horizontal heat transport are disregarded.

Recent experiments with combined atmosphere–ocean models have been carried out by the National Oceanic and Atmospheric Administration (NOAA) Geophysical Fluid Dynamics Laboratory (GFDL), the National Aeronautics and Space Administration (NASA) Goddard Institute for Space Studies (GISS), Oregon State University (OSU), and the Lawrence Livermore Laboratory (LLL) (with a two–dimensional model). The National Center for Atmospheric Research (NCAR) has used some simple models to study the effects of carbon dioxide and is currently in the process of running a more complete coupled three–dimensional atmosphere-ocean model in a carbon dioxide experiment. (Descriptions of several of these efforts are given in Appendix B.)

The way such models are used in these kinds of experiments deserves some comment. The procedure is to first run the model with current boundary conditions for a long enough period (in model time) so that the model's climate is established. It can then be compared with the real climate. This is the "control run." If the model involves a time–dependent GCM of the atmosphere coupled to an ocean model, it is important that the combined model be run long enough to obtain all the statistics necessary to characterize climate, including the *variability* or "noise" of the important parameters. If this is not done properly, the results will be inconclusive (Chervin and Schneider, 1976; Chervin, 1980).

The next step in the experiment is to run the model again with increased carbon dioxide concentration, usually double or quadruple the present value. This is called the "perturbed run." All other factors and boundary conditions (with some exceptions) remain the same as in the control run. The differences between the control run and the perturbed run are then presented and compared with the model noise. If these differences ("signals") are larger than the model variability ("noise") the results of the experiment are considered statistically significant.

Primarily, results have been presented in terms of temperature, both globally averaged and as a function of latitude (sometimes as a function of longitude as well). If the model includes a suitable hydrological cycle, results can also be presented in terms of precipitation, evaporation, and even soil moisture.

A brief review of the various models, their main characteristics, and the results of carbon dioxide experiments with them are

41

presented in Appendix B. All but one of the experiments with atmosphere–ocean climate models gave increases of 1.5°C to 4°C for the globally averaged surface temperature warming ( $\Delta T_s$ ) due to a doubling of carbon dioxide. They showed a somewhat larger cooling of the entire stratosphere. (The exception was the initial OSU experiment, in which ocean temperature distribution was arbitrarily and unrealistically held at the current seasonal values; therefore the response was, predictably, very much smaller.) Polar temperature changes were generally larger than the average by a factor of about two or three in the Northern Hemisphere, but less in the Southern Hemisphere. Comparing seasonal temperature changes at middle and high northern latitudes, the reported warmings are larger in winter than in summer. It is claimed that this is primarily due to the influence of the Arctic sea ice and snowcover on land (Manabe, private communication). Both the GFDL and GISS experiments show a reduced global response when seasonally varying insolation is used instead of an annual average with no seasons.

None of the climate models that have been used in these carbon dioxide experiments have truly coupled and interacting oceans. The reason is that none of the ocean submodels here treat ocean heat transport as a factor that varies with atmospheric circulation and changing wind stress. However, work is proceeding at NCAR, GFDL, and OSU (and probably elsewhere) toward improved coupled models, and we will soon be able to see how much difference this ocean transport factor makes in the results. Furthermore, the large thermal capacity of the oceans may introduce as much as a two-decade lag in the response of the atmospheric system (NAS, 1979; Schneider and Thompson, 1980). This factor has not been adequately studied.

Some have feared that variable cloudiness could be a potentially large feedback mechanism that might greatly modify the response of the atmospheric system. However, other studies now indicate that the net effect of cloudiness changes could be quite small, and would not necessarily affect the atmosphere significantly. These studies include investigations based on satellite observations (Cess, 1976), which show cloudiness changes in the real atmosphere, and experiments with models in which cloudiness is calculated together with its effect on the shortwave (solar) and longwave (terrestrial) radiation balance (Schneider, Washington, and Chervin, 1978; Manabe and Wetherald, 1980). Nevertheless, this matter deserves further attention.

We must emphasize that much insight can be gained from studies with simpler types of models. The earliest estimates of the globally averaged climatic effect of carbon dioxide increase were with one-dimensional radiative–convective models (e.g., Manabe and Wetherald, 1967). Subsequently latitude–dependent and zonally averaged energy–balanced models were used to explore many aspects of the climate system, including the effects of carbon dioxide. The advantage of such models is that individual factors and feedback mechanisms can be isolated and analyzed without the large computer time required for GCMs. Reviews of these hierarchies of models describe their features and applications in more detail than we can include here (e.g., Schneider and Dickinson, 1974; Ramanathan and Coakley, 1978; Ramanathan, Lian, and Cess, 1979). It is now recognized that the development of a more complete climate theory requires research using both the simpler and the more complex models.

## 3.2 Studies of past climate changes

Geological formations and sediments on ocean and lake bottoms contain clues to the Earth's past climates. We will discuss in more detail later how the information on past warmer periods might give us insight into the future. But the point to make here is that scientists can and do take advantage of the natural record to study climatic change (WMO, 1979a).

There are a variety of approaches to this kind of study that are pertinent to the carbon dioxide effect, as pointed out by Flohn (1979) and others (WMO, 1979b). The more obvious approaches should try to determine the following:

- The anomalous patterns of temperature and precipitation that prevailed during the five or ten warmest years in the period of good synoptic meteorological observation (Wigley et al., 1979; Williams, 1979);
- Whether there were distinctive patterns of temperature and precipitation during the warm period, 1935–1950;
- What these patterns were during the warm period of Viking exploration, from 900–1200;
- The precipitation patterns that prevailed at various times during the Altithermal (or Hypsithermal) Period, 4500 to 8000 years ago when the average global temperature appears to have been 2°C to 4°C warmer than now (Kellogg, 1977; 1978; Flohn and Nicholson, 1980; Butzer, 1980);
- The conditions during the last interglacial — that is, the period

between ice ages — the Eemian–Sangamon Period some 110,000 years ago. It appears to have been warmer than the present Holocene interglacial, suggested by the fact that sea level was 5 to 6 meters higher than now. One or more of the existing ice sheets may have been smaller (see Section 3.3);

● What a much warmer Earth would be like, one without permanent ice at either pole, such as in the Tertiary Period more than 20 million years ago, a time before Antarctica acquired its ice sheets. Flohn (1979) has pointed out that between about 20 million and 5 million years ago there was a marked asymmetry in the climate system due to the fact that the southern polar regions had become glaciated and the northern polar regions had not (Herman and Hopkins, 1980). This situation could recur because of a carbon dioxide-induced warming, making general circulation patterns very different.

### 3.3 The cryosphere's response to climatic change

The polar regions deserve attention for at least three reasons. First, most climate models suggest that climate changes will be greatest in the polar regions (see Section 3.1 and Appendix B). Observations also suggest that the size of the cryosphere is particularly sensitive to temperature and precipitation changes (Barry, 1979). Second, feedback mechanisms between the cryosphere, atmosphere, and oceans would affect the climate outside the polar regions. Third, substantial change in ice sheet volume would affect sea levels with potentially drastic consequences for shoreline areas.

Two modeling studies of the perennial Arctic Ocean ice pack suggest that the ice may disappear entirely in the summertime with the warming that would accompany a doubling of carbon dioxide. But the ice would reappear in at least part of the ocean in winter (Manabe and Stouffer, 1979; Parkinson and Kellogg, 1979). This would probably have serious consequences for the climate of the entire Arctic Basin (Fletcher et al., 1973); and it further substantiates the need for monitoring the ice pack there (ICEX, 1979).

Special attention is being given to the continental ice sheets, partly because one of the most dramatic consequences of a global warming would be the partial melting or disintegration of these ice sheets and subsequent rises in sea level. A rise of 5 to 6 meters would result if the entire West Antarctic ice sheet melted, and a similar amount if the Greenland ice sheet melted. If the East Antarctic ice sheet melted sea level could rise by an additional 60 meters, but that is not considered possible in the next thousand years or more.

The West Antarctic ice sheet and portions of the East Antarctic ice sheet are grounded below sea level and have associated ice shelves, apparently holding them in place. Some glaciologists have postulated that if these ice shelves disappeared the massive ice sheets they buttress could begin to slide into the sea. Conceivably this could happen if the oceans warmed somewhat, but the time scale on which it would occur — decades, centuries, or millennia — is still uncertain (Radok, 1978; Bentley, 1980).

## 3.4 Conclusions concerning future climate

To summarize what has been said, there is little doubt that an increase in atmospheric carbon dioxide concentration will result in a general warming of the lower atmosphere and a cooling of the stratosphere. The best climate models tested to date that simulate warming due to a doubling of carbon dioxide suggest a global average temperature rise of between 1.5° and 4°C (roughly 3° ± 1.5°C). This change may occur in the first half of the next century, perhaps later; it is considerably larger than any natural climate changes that have occurred in the past several thousand years. The response in the polar regions will be greater than the average by a factor of about two or three in the Northern Hemisphere, and greater in winter than in summer. The response of the Southern Hemisphere will probably be less due to the relatively larger ocean area and the stability from season to season of the Antarctic snowcover.

These results pertain to carbon dioxide increase alone, but it is important to take into account a likely increase of several other long lasting infrared–absorbing gases that we add to the atmosphere. These gases (ozone, methane, chlorofluoromethanes, carbon monoxide, nitrous oxide, etc.) could contribute as much as another 50 percent to the greenhouse effect from carbon dioxide.

This general warming will be accompanied by a weakening of the temperature differences between the equator and the poles, which will affect the general circulation — though exactly how is still unclear. The kinetic energy of the atmosphere may be less, and this will in turn reduce the average wind stress on the oceans, thereby modifying ocean circulations as well.

For various reasons, the polar regions require special attention. Several theoretical studies suggest that the Arctic Ocean ice pack could disappear entirely in summer with a carbon dioxide doubling, affecting the entire Arctic Basin climate. The habitability and ecology of vast areas at high latitudes in the Northern Hemisphere would be affected, since the warming would affect the distribution of snowcover and permafrost. Finally, the possibility that ice sheets (particularly the West Antarctic one) could shrink or begin to disintegrate suggests that sea level might rise by several meters. However, glaciologists cannot yet agree on what time scale this process would take place.

Based on current knowledge, these are some of the main conclusions that can be drawn concerning the climatic effects of increased carbon dioxide. The picture of the future, however, is far from clear. There are many gaps in our understanding of the behavior of the climate system.

Climate research should take several directions in order to increase our understanding and ability to draw credible scenarios of the future climate. NAS and WMO have recommended that the following receive high priority (NAS, 1979; WMO, 1979b):

- Coupling ocean models that include heat transport to atmospheric models that include variable cloudiness;
- Including in climate models as completely as possible the physical processes at the land surface that control such variables as albedo, soil moisture, and water runoff;
- Reconstructing the record of past warmer climates. There are a number of such periods that should be studied, each with its special features (see Section 3.2) — though presumably each had a somewhat different cause. Insight into conditions on a warmer planet and a possible check on results with climate models can both be gained;
- Studying the response of the cryosphere to a warming, with emphasis on the Arctic sea ice and the ice sheets of Greenland and the Antarctic (see Section 3.3);
- Monitoring the volumes and movements of ice sheets using satellite remote sensing. In this way ice sheet modelers and glaciologists may be able to predict the behavior of the ice sheets (Brooks et al., 1978; ICEX, 1979);
- Describing *regional and seasonal* changes of temperature, precipitation, and soil moisture. This difficult task would rely on the latest results of both climate model experiments and reconstructions of past climates. It is one way that scenarios of future climate can be made useful for studies of how climatic change will affect human activities. The next section discusses these scenarios in more detail.

## 4. Climate Scenarios: Windows on the Future

From what has been said above about the many uncertainties in our knowledge of the response of the climate system to an increase in atmospheric carbon dioxide, it appears to be a futile exercise at this time to try to make a *detailed prediction* of what the future warmer Earth will be like. As depicted in Figure I.2 and discussed in the preceeding section, we simply do not know enough about all the interacting factors that will be involved, particularly future human behavior.

But we are still trying to understand what the impacts of future climate variations and change will be on society since politicians, business people, economists, agronomists, engineers, and other policy makers and planners need a clear picture of what kind of environmental changes to expect — or, at least, the range of possibilities.

This creates a dilemma: Climatologists are still unable to make a detailed prediction of the future climate; yet without such a prediction we cannot study the societal responses and alternative choices ahead. One solution to this dilemma is to compose a set of *climate scenarios* that describe the patterns of seasonal and regional weather that could occur on a warmer Earth. Climatologists would probably not be able to agree on which scenario is the most likely to actually unfold, but they should not be suprised if any one turned out to be true — they are all "surprise-free scenarios" (Kahn et al., 1976).

As we pointed out in the preceding section, there are a number of approaches climatologists could take in drawing up such climate scenarios, and all should be pursued. They include examining the following:

- Results of experiments with various kinds of climate models, in particular the coupled GCM–ocean models;
- Patterns of weather and climate that have occurred during the past 100 years or so;
- Reconstructions of warmer periods in the past.

Such climate scenarios, to be of any real value in impact studies, should provide at least the following information concerning an Earth with, say, doubled atmospheric carbon dioxide:

- Regional and seasonal patterns of *mean temperature and precipitation or soil moisture.* (For agricultural purposes the growing season is obviously very important.) These are probably most easily comprehended if presented in the form of maps of deviations from the present mean conditions — warmer or cooler, wetter or drier;
- Indications of the *variability* from year to year of the daily,

weekly, or monthly mean weather conditions. This will probably be harder to specify than the means, but the variations or extreme events — that is droughts, cold or hot spells, and floods — most directly affect our lives. These must eventually be taken into account in impact studies.

In Figure II.3 we present a partial and tentative example of a climatic scenario in which deviations from present growing season soil moisture are plotted for the world. Appendix C discusses sources on which this map is based. It will be seen that there were a good many inputs available — often conflicting, unfortunately. The lessons and caveats to be learned from this first scenario–drawing exercise need to be emphasized:

- Evidence on which climate scenarios must be based is fragmentary and often contradictory;
- There are some regions of the world where most indications tend to be in agreement. It is reasonable to assign a higher probability to the specified climate change occurring in those regions, as we have done in Figure II.3;
- The fact that drier or wetter climatic conditions existed during past warmer periods does not guarantee that the same conditions will reoccur in the future if the Earth is warmed by the carbon dioxide greenhouse effect. There are going to be many boundary conditions that are different, such as the distribution of snow and ice, sea surface temperatures, and patterns of vegetation and deserts. These differences will influence the large scale circulations that determine regional temperature and precipitation;
- We have a few hints concerning the variability of the patterns shown in a scenario, and arguments can be made for a decrease of variability. For example, one might say that it could be more "summerlike" on a warmer Earth and that therefore there would be a weaker general circulation and fewer extreme events. Indeed variability of the current weather is known to be less in summer than in winter (Madden and Ramanathan, 1980). Furthermore, experience with climate model experiments also suggests that the variability will be less with increased carbon dioxide (Wetherald, personal communication). Thus, while future variability of the weather from day to day and year to year may be less than now, this point needs to be established more firmly and eventually determined on a regional basis.

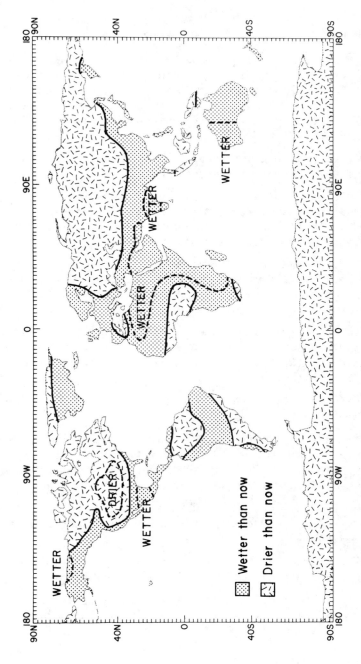

Figure II.3. Example of a scenario of possible soil moisture patterns on a warmer Earth. It is based on paleoclimatic reconstructions of the Altithermal Period (4500 to 8000 years ago), comparisons of recent warm and cold years in the Northern Hemisphere, and a climate model experiment. (For a discussion of these sources of information see Appendix C.) Where two or more of these sources agree on the direction of the change we have indicated the area of agreement with a dashed line and a label.

# REFERENCES

Arrhenius, S. 1903: *Lehrbuch der kosmischen Physik 2*, Hirzel, Leipzig.

Bacastow, R.B. and C.D. Keeling, 1973: Atmospheric carbon dioxide and radiocarbon in the natural carbon cycle: Changes from A.D. 1700 to 2070 as deduced from a geochemical model. In *Carbon and the Biosphere*, G.M. Woodwell and E.V. Pecan (eds.), U.S. Atomic Energy Commission, Washington D.C. (CONF-720510), 86–135.

Barrett, E.W., 1975: Inadvertent weather and climate modification. *Critical Revs. Environ. Control* 6, 15–90.

Barry R. 1979: Cryospheric responses to global temperature increase. In *Proceedings of the DOE Workshop on the Global Effects of Carbon Dioxide from Fossil Fuels*, U.S. Dept. of Energy, Washington, D.C. (CONF-770385.)

Bentley, C.R., 1980: Response of the West Antarctic ice sheet to $CO_2$–induced climatic warming. Report of DOE sponsored meeting at Orono, Maine, June (to be published as part of a AAAS study report).

Berner, W., H. Oeschger, and B. Stauffer, 1980: Information on the $CO_2$ cycle from ice core studies, *Proceedings of the 10th International Radiocarbon Conference*, Bern and Heidelberg, August 1979 (in press).

Björkstrom, A., 1979a: Man's global redistribution of carbon. *Ambio* 8, 254–259.

Björkstrom, A., 1979b: A model of $CO_2$ interaction between atmosphere, oceans, and land biota. In SCOPE No. 13, Scientific Committee on Problems of the Environment, International Council of Scientific Unions, Wiley, New York, 403–456.

Bolin, B. and W. Bischof, 1970: Variations in the carbon dioxide content of the atmosphere of the northern hemisphere. *Tellus* 22, 431–442.

Broecker, W.S., 1975: Climatic change: Are we on the brink of a pronounced global warming? *Science* 189, 460–463.

Broecker, W.S., T. Takahashi, H.J. Simpson and T.H. Peng, 1979: Fate of fossil fuel carbon dioxide and the global carbon budget. *Science* 206, 409–418.

Brooks, R.L., W.J. Campbell, R.O. Ramseier, H.R. Stanley and H.J. Zwally, 1978: Ice sheet topography by satellite altimetry. *Nature* 274, 539–543.

Butzer, K., 1980: Adaptation to global environmental change. *Prof. Geographer*, 32, 269–278.

Callendar, G.S., 1958: On the amount of carbon dioxide in the atmosphere. *Tellus* 10, 243–248.

Cess, R.D., 1976: Climate change: An appraisal of atmospheric feedback mechanisms employing zonal climatology. *J. Atmos. Sci.* 33, 1831–1843.

Chamberlain, T.C., 1899: An attempt to frame a working hypothesis of the cause of glacial epochs on an atmospheric basis. *J. Geology*, 7.

Chervin, R.M., 1980: On the simulation of climate and climate change with general circulation models. *J. Atmos. Sci.* (Sept. issue, in press).

Chervin, R.M. and S.H. Schneider, 1976: On the determination of statistical significance of climate experiments with general circulation models. *J. Atmos. Sci.* 33, 405–412.

Delmas, R. J., J. –M. Ascencio, and M. Legrand, 1980: Polar ice evidence that atmospheric $CO_2$ 20,000 years BP was 50% of present. *Nature* 284, 155–157.

Fletcher, J.O., Y. Mintz, A. Arakawa and T. Fox, 1973: Numerical simulation of the influence of Arctic sea ice on climate. In *Energy Fluxes over Polar Surfaces* (Proc. IAMAP/IAPSO/SCAR/WMO Symposium, Moscow, August 1971), WMO Tech. Note No. 129, World Meteorological Organization, Geneva, 181–218.

Flohn, H., 1979: A scenario of possible future climates — natural and man-made. In *Proceedings of the World Climate Conference*, WMO No. 537, World Meteorological Organization, Geneva, 243–268.

Flohn, H. and S. Nicholson, 1980: Climatic fluctuations in the arid belt of the "Old World" since the last glacial maximum: Possible causes and future implications. In *Palaeoecology of Africa and the Surrounding Islands* 12, E.M. Van Zinderen Bakkerand and J.A. Coetzee eds., A.A. Balkema, Rotterdam,Netherlands, 3–21.

Hameed, S., R.D. Cess, and J.S. Hogan, 1980: Response of the global climate to changes in atmospheric chemical composition due to fossil fuel burning. *J. Geophys. Res.* (in press).

Herman, Y. and D.M. Hopkins, 1980: Arctic Ocean climate in late Cenozoic time. *Science* 209, 557–562.

ICEX, 1979: *Ice and Climate Experiment.* Rept. of Science and Applications Working Group, Goddard Space Flight Cntr., NASA, Greenbelt, Md.

IIASA, 1978: *Carbon Dioxide, Climate and Society.* J. Williams (ed.), International Institute for Applied Systems Analysis, Laxenburg, Austria, Pergamon Press, New York.

Kahn, H., W. Brown and L. Martel, 1976: *The Next 200 Years,* Wm. Morrow, New York.

Keeling, C.D., R.B. Bacastow, A.E. Bainbridge, C.A. Ekdahl, P.R. Guenther and L.S. Waterman, 1976a: Atmospheric carbon dioxide variations at Mauna Loa Observatory, Hawaii. *Tellus* 28, 538–551.

Keeling, C.D., J.A. Adams, C.A. Ekdahl, and P.R. Guenther, 1976b: Atmospheric carbon dioxide variations at the South Pole. *Tellus* 28, 552–564.

Keeling, C.D. and R.B. Bacastow, 1977: Impact of industrial gases on climate. In *Energy and Climate,* Geophysics Research Board, National Academy of Sciences, Washington, D.C., 72–95.

Kellogg, W.W., 1977: *Effects of Human Activities on Global Climate.* WMO Tech. Note No. 156, World Meteorological Organization, Geneva, Switzerland.

Kellogg, W.W., 1978: Global influences of mankind on climate. In *Climatic Change,* J. Gribbin (ed.), Cambridge University Press, Cambridge, 205–227.

Kellogg, W.W., 1979: Influences of mankind on climate. *Ann. Rev. Earth Planet. Sci. 7,* 63–92.

Kellogg, W.W. and S.H. Schneider 1974: Climate stabilization: For better or for worse? *Science* 186, 1163–1172.

Kerr, R.A., 1980: Carbon budget not so out of whack. *Science* 208, 1358–1359.

Llewellyn, R. A. and W. M. Washington, 1977: Effluents of energy production: Regional and global aspects. In *Energy and Climate*, Geophysics Research Board, National Academy of Sciences, Washington, D.C.

Machta, L., 1973: Prediction of $CO_2$ in the atmosphere. In *Carbon and the Biosphere*, G.M. Woodwell and E.V. Pecan (eds.), U.S. Atomic Energy Commission Washington, D.C. (CONF–720510), 21–31.

Madden, R. A. and V. Ramanathan, 1980: Detecting climate change due to increasing carbon dioxide. *Science* 209, 763–768.

Manabe, S. and R. T. Wetherald, 1967: Thermal equilibrium of the atmosphere with a given distribution of relative humidity. *J. Atmos. Sci.* 24, 241–259.

Manabe, S. and R. Stouffer, 1979: A $CO_2$–climate sensitivity study with a mathematical model of global climate. *Nature* 282, 491–493.

Manabe, S. and R. T. Wetherald, 1980: On the distribution of climate change resulting from an increase in $CO_2$ content of the atmosphere. *J. Atmos. Sci.* 37, 99–118.

NAS, 1977: *Energy and Climate*. Studies in Geophysics, National Academy of Sciences, Washington, D.C.

NAS, 1979: *Carbon Dioxide and Climate: A Scientific Assessment*. Report of ad hoc Study Group on Carbon Dioxide and Climate, Woods Hole, Mass., Climate Research Board, National Academy of Sciences, Washington, D.C.

NOAA, 1975: *Geophysical Monitoring for Climatic Change*. J.M. Miller (ed.), No. 3, Summary Rept. 1974, Environ. Res. Labs., Natl. Oceanic and Atmos. Admin., Boulder, Colo.

Parkinson, C.L. and W.W. Kellogg, 1979: Arctic sea ice decay simulated for $CO_2$–induced temperature rise. *Climatic Change* 2, 149–162.

Radok, U., 1978: *Climatic Roles of Ice*. Tech. Doc. on Hydrology, Intl. Hydrol. Progr., UNESCO, Paris.

Ramanathan, V., 1980: Climatic effects of anthropogenic trace gases. In *Interactions of Energy and Climate*, W. Bach, J. Pankrath, and J. Williams (eds.), Reidel, Dordrecht, Netherlands, 269–280.

Ramanathan, V. and J.A. Coakley, 1978: Climate modeling through radiative–convective models. *Rev. Geophys. Space Phys.* 16, 465–489.

Ramanathan, V., M.S. Lian, and R.D. Cess, 1979: Increased atmospheric $CO_2$: Zonal and seasonal estimates of the effect on the radiation energy balance and surface temperature. *J. Geophys. Res.* 84, 4947–4958.

Revelle, R. and W. Munk, 1977: The carbon dioxide cycle and the biosphere. In *Energy and Climate*, Geophysics Research Board, Naitonal Academy of Sciences, Washington, D.C., 140–158.

Rotty, R.M., 1979: Energy demand and global climate change. In *Man's Impact on Climate.*, W. Bach, J. Pankrath, and W.W. Kellogg (eds.), Developments in Atmospheric Science 10, Elsevier, Amsterdam, 269–283.

Schneider, S.H. and R. E. Dickinson, 1974: Climate modeling. *Rev. Geophys. Space Phys.* 12, 447–493.

Schneider, S.H., W.M. Washington and R.M. Chervin, 1978: Cloudiness as a climatic feedback mechanism: Effects on cloud amounts of prescribed global and regional surface temperature changes in the NCAR GCM. *J. Atmos. Sci.* 35, 2207–2221.

Schneider, S. H. and S. L. Thompson, 1980: Atmospheric $CO_2$ and climate: Importance of the transient response. *J. Geophys. Res.* (in press).

SCOPE, 1979: *The Global Carbon Cycle.* B. Bolin, E.T. Degens, S. Kempe and P. Ketner (eds.), SCOPE No. 13, Scientific Committee on Problems of the Environment, International Council of Scientific Unions, Wiley, New York.

Seiler, W. and P. J. Crutzen, 1980: Estimates of gross and net fluxes of carbon between the biosphere and the atmosphere from biomass burning. *Climatic Change* 2, 207–247.

Siegenthaler, U. and H. Oeschger, 1978: Predicting future atmospheric carbon dioxide levels. *Science* 199, 388–395.

SMIC, 1971: *Inadvertent Climate Modification: Report of the Study of Man's Impact on Climate.* M.I.T. Press, Cambridge, Mass.

Sommer, A., 1976: Attempt at an assessment of the world's tropical moist forests. *Unasylva*, Food and Agriculture Organization, Rome, 28, 5–25.

Stuiver, M., 1978: Atmospheric carbon dioxide and carbon reservoir changes. *Science* 199, 253–258.

TIE, 1980: *The role of Organic Soils in the World Carbon Cycle – Problem Analysis and Research Needs,* T.V. Armentano (ed.), The Institute of Ecology, Indianapolis, Indiana, UC–11, Dept. of Energy, Washington, D.C. (CONF–7905135).

Wigley, T.M.E., P.D. Jones and P.M. Kelly, 1979: Scenario for a warm, high–$CO_2$ world. *Nature* 283, 17–20.

Williams, J., 1979: Anomalies in temperature and rainfall during warm Arctic seasons as a guide to the formulation of climate scenarios. *Climatic Change* 2, 249–266.

Williams, J., G. Krömer and A. Gilchrist, 1979: The impact of waste heat release on climate: Experiments with a general circulation model, *J. Appl. Meteor.* 18, 1501–1511.

WMO, 1979a: *Proceedings of the World Climate Conference,* WMO No. 537, World Meteorological Organization, Geneva.

WMO 1979b: *Report of the Meeting of CAS Working Group on Atmospheric Carbon Dioxide.* Boulder, Colo., November, 1979, WMO Proj. on Res. and Monitoring of $CO_2$, Rept. No. 2, World Meteorological Organization, Geneva. (See Appendix C of Report No. 2).

Woodwell, G.M., R.H. Whittaker, W.A. Reiners, G.E. Likens, C.C. Delwiche and D.B. Botkin, 1978: The biota and the world carbon budget. *Science* 199, 141–146.

Zimen, K.E., P. Offerman, and G. Hartmann, 1977: Source functions of $CO_2$ and future $CO_2$ burden in the atmosphere. *Zeit. Naturforschung* 32a, 1544–1554.

# III.  IMPACTS OF CLIMATIC CHANGE

## 1.  Nature and Methods of Impact Studies

How climate interacts with society is extraordinarily complex. Methods to assess these interactions are just beginning to be developed through interdisciplinary studies. In its proposed "Outline Plan and Basis for the World Climate Programme 1980–1983," the World Meteorological Organization (WMO, 1980) notes:

> A full assessment of climatic impact must trace its consequences well into the economic and social fabric of society and examine the whole complexity of linkages and feedbacks in climatic impacts on the biosphere and on human activities. In this connection, analysis of sensitivity of climate/society interactions are among the most important tasks to be undertaken.

Carbon dioxide–induced climatic impacts may affect many aspects of human activity, as illustrated in Figure I.2. The activities we consider most closely related to the carbon dioxide problem include: energy supply and demand; world food production; biomes of all types; water resources; fisheries and marine resources; human health, disease, and comfort; population settlements; and tourism and recreation.

In our view, the ultimate objective of carbon dioxide/climate impact studies should be to decrease the vulnerability of these activities and increase our ability to respond and adjust to the impact. The WMO (1980) recommends specific aims that impact studies should strive for:

- Improving our knowledge of the impact of climatic change in terms of primary responses of natural and human systems;
- Developing our knowledge and awareness of the interaction between climatic variability and change and human activities;
- Improving such methods as case studies and models to better understand interactions among the climate, environment, and society;
- Determining the characteristics of human societies at different levels of development and in different environments that make them either especially vulnerable or especially resilient to climatic change, and that also permit

them to take advantage of the opportunities posed by such changes.

In order to achieve these aims, at least three major steps must be taken in future studies: clarify the underlying assumptions and value judgments in climatic impact assessments; analyze the most useful models of climatic impact assessment; and refine the methods used to estimate the relative political, economic, and social costs of alternative strategies to mitigate the effects of climatic impacts.

## 1.1 Cost/benefit analyses

Ideally we would like to present decision makers with data on the costs and risks of the climatic change in store for each region and its various activities, and show how costs would change with alternative programs of action. These kinds of assessments in market economies are generally called cost/benefit analyses (d'Arge, 1979; Smith, 1980).

One ingredient of such analyses is an estimate of the *discount rates* that will prevail in the decades ahead. The discount rate can be defined as the expected rate at which a capital investment will pay for itself. An appropriate example for the carbon dioxide problem would be to determine how much we would have to invest now to safeguard, say, natural resources for the future. This permits us to evaluate future needs and opportunities, thereby extending the options for future generations.

The choice of discount rates may vary between private and public sectors, and with the mechanisms that govern international markets — mechanisms that can be expected to change with time. For instance, long term considerations are usually distinct from the discount rates commonly adopted for public and private investments. Economists are already studying how people feel about endowing future generations (d'Arge et al., 1980). This is a first step in refining the assessment of risk required for impact studies.

A major source of uncertainty about the future costs and benefits of climatic change arises when economic methodologies are applied to the problem. There is a continuing debate about how well traditional economic analysis can deal with long term climatic impact studies. The Climate Impacts Assessment Program (CIAP), sponsored by the Department of Transportation, estimated the national costs of a climatic change due to a hypothetical fleet of supersonic transport aircraft (d'Arge et al., 1975). This approach was subsequently used in a study (d'Arge et al., 1976; d'Arge, 1979) of the costs of controlling chlorofluoromethane in spray can propellants, refrigerators, and air conditioners in order to protect the ozone layer. Hence, given certain assumptions, an economic cost/benefit analysis can be made of an environmental change and the costs of controlling it.

However, Smith (1980) points out that:

As we traverse the road from theoretical (economic) ideals to practice it is easy to enumerate circumstances in which the production or consumption processes for a good or service have special attributes not reflected by market prices, or the actions governed by markets lead to effects that are either external or unintentional by-products of the decisions involved.

This could be summarized by saying that many important goods or services in our lives cannot be assigned a price tag, and that our economic and social structures do not remain fixed over an extended period, which makes economic predictions difficult. This is especially pertinent to a world with a changing climate.

Hence, conventional economic tools such as cost/benefit analyses are still poorly suited for assessing the long term consequences of climate change. The difficulty with extending an economic assessment over several decades is that economic and social values will probably not remain fixed; there may be unforeseen societal changes.

## 1.2 Preparing for the impacts

Even if our economic tools remain inadequate to predict the future, there is considerable practical experience in dealing with a variable climate now. There are many operations that must take into account a range of weather conditions; among them are agriculture, water supply, and utilities supplying gas and oil. Since we cannot predict weather or climate more than a season ahead, some flexibility must be built into any climate sensitive operation, even though this will usually involve added costs (Stigler, 1939; McFadden, 1980). We will stress this again in some of the following sections.

The point to emphasize here is that the methods for dealing with a variable climate can be applied to long term climate change. The techniques we use to cope with variable climate now add flexibility to our economic and social systems; this flexibility should help to mitigate the effects of a slow, long term climate change. Furthermore, the basic methodologies for dealing with variable climate are already established and used in many operations. Thus, dealing with climate variability (and, consequently, climate change)

59

is by no means a new subject to planners in agriculture, industry, and government.

Even though climatic variablity has been recognized as an important factor in planning, it is often not properly taken into account. Heady et al. (1973) have shown that when using agricultural production models to assess U.S. crop output, 223 different production areas for field crops must be taken into account. In each area there is a range of water availability and management alternatives. Howe (1980) emphasizes the importance of considering the variety of ways water supplies are managed:

> ... the identification of the impacts of climate variability must be fine tuned to local conditions, as must the design of strategies to mitigate negative impacts. It suggests that the effects of longer term climate change may also differ substantially at local levels, so that research on adaptation to changing climate will have to take local and regional differences into account.

In this case Howe was referring to Colorado, where the mountains cause large climatic differences from place to place. This situation also exists in many other parts of the world.

Seen in its broadest context, then, the tools that are available to assess the impacts of climate variability and change must be adapted to the process of deciding which strategies will best mitigate the impacts. These tools are not suitable for predicting the future, even given the kind of climate scenario described in Section II.4. Rather, they are for the use of planners in choosing among alternatives. Economists are generally aware of their limitations as well as their capabilities (Smith, 1980).

## 2. Energy Supply and Demand

A large portion of global energy demand is in the developed world, located for the most part in temperate latitudes. The greatest single use of energy in these areas is for space heating and cooling. Hence, variations of climate can influence energy demand. Climate also affects demand by determining how much energy will be needed to pump water for irrigation, since this depends on rainfall.

Climate affects energy supply as well. Recent extreme climatic events — the harsh winter of 1976–77 in the United States, for example — both increased energy demand and curtailed energy supplies.

In this section we will explore the climatic impact on energy supply and demand, and discuss ways to prepare for future long term climatic

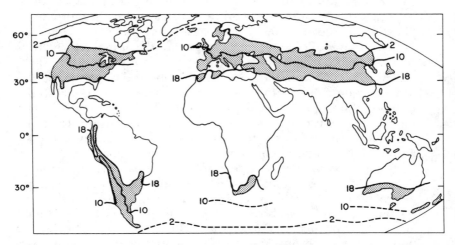

**Figure III.1.** **Mean annual temperature. The shaded area lies between 2°C and 18°C, where the maximum demand for space heating occurs (McKay and Allsopp, 1980).**

change based on the lessons gained from past short term climatic fluctuations.

### 2.1 Climate and energy demand

The energy required to maintain comfortable living conditions is markedly affected by climate. When it is cold, heat must be supplied; when it is hot, air conditioners are needed. It is estimated that in the U.S., 18 percent of the total annual energy demand is for space heating, in Canada, 29 percent, and in Denmark 50 percent (McKay and Allsopp, 1980).

The maximum use of space heating closely follows the 10°C mean annual temperature isotherm, shown in Figure III.1. At warmer temperatures the demand per capita is less, virtually ceasing at 18°C mean temperature; so few people live poleward of the 2°C mean temperature isotherm that total energy demand for heating there is also negligible. Notice that the industrial areas in both hemispheres, where energy demand is the greatest, lie in the shaded area between 2°C and 18°C. In a carbon dioxide–induced climate change, these two bands would generally shift poleward.

While the energy demand for heating correlates with outside temperatures it is also dependent on buildings' insulation, exposure to the Sun, and heating management. One useful way to relate energy demand and temperature is to calculate the number of "heating degree days" in a month. Heating degree days are defined as the number of degrees the average monthly temperature drops below a certain base temperature (taken variously to be 15°C, 18°C, 18.3°C, or 19°C) multiplied by the number of days in the month. Monthly energy demand for heating is nearly proportional to the number of heating degree days in the month, though there may be differences from one community or country to another. The same approach can be used to estimate energy demands for air conditioning, although in this case humidity may have to be considered as well as temperature. Also note that the energy demand for air conditioning is for electricity rather than gas or oil.

We have recently experienced unusually cold winters with heating demands far above average. For example, in the United States the November 1976 to March 1977 heating season had 22 percent more heating degree days than the preceeding years (corresponding to a 1.8°C drop in seasonally averaged temperatures) (Quirk and Moriarty, 1980; National Climatic Center, 1979). The result was a natural gas and fuel oil shortage in the Northeast, since the utilities and pipeline companies were not prepared for the extra demand. This caused general hardship and unemployment for up to one million workers by February, 1977.

That same winter the rainy season in California was much drier than usual, and water allotments to agriculture were reduced by 60 percent. In a normal year 85 percent of the fresh water supply in California is used for crops. Consequently, farmers were forced to replace the deficit by pumping up more ground water for irrigation. Statewide the energy required for this operation was about 1 billion kilowatt hours, which cost California farmers over $25 million (House of Representatives, 1978).

Altogether, it is estimated that energy related losses to the United States gross national product in the winter of 1976–1977 amounted to $20 billion (McKay and Allsopp, 1980). We should note that the cold in the eastern part of the country and the drought in the western part were caused by the same pattern of the large scale general circulation: a persistent ridge of high pressure in the west and a trough of low pressure in the east. This kind of shift of the semi–permanent ridges and troughs could occur again; we can expect other shifts to occur during long term climate changes that would have major influences on regional climate (see Section II.3).

Transportation, which accounts for about 26 percent of all

energy use in the United States, is also affected by adverse weather. There are a number of other industries such as construction and tourism that are sensitive to rain, snow, or extreme temperatures. However, the influence of weather and climate on these activities is hard to quantify because of the many nonclimatic factors that come into play.

The above examples of climatic impacts on the United States are all due to extreme, short lived anomalies that caused temporary hardships and unexpected costs. We can learn from these events how to cope with variable climate, but dealing with a more gradual, long term change is likely to be quite different. For instance, given enough time to prepare, agriculture and industry probably can adapt by modifying their practices. Furthermore, rising costs of energy will tend to reduce demand; people will be more willing to conserve. In other words, economic and social forces as well as climate will shape future energy demand.

## 2.2  Climate and energy supply

The winter of 1977–1978 was almost as cold as the preceding one, which we have just described. However, in 1977–1978 there were virtually no fuel shortages or weather related unemployment. Thus it seems that American industry probably had adequate energy supplies for unusually cold winters, but it was just unprepared to distribute them in 1976–1977 (Quirk and Moriarty, 1980).

While planning was partly to blame for fuel shortages in 1976–1977 (not enough fuel reserves were on hand), climate contributed to the disruption of the supply flow in many ways: A drop of natural gas pressure in storage areas due to the cold left utilities with insufficient pumping capacity to retrieve the stored gas; barges loaded with coal were stranded in frozen waterways; and piles of coal outside power plants were too frozen to dig out (Quirk and Moriarty, 1980). Once the problems were recognized it was possible to draw up contingency plans to deal with them.

Energy supplies might be bolstered if renewable energy resources were developed; there are persuasive reasons for pushing such developments as fast as possible (Lovins, 1980; Sorenson, 1975). But some renewable sources may be more vulnerable to vagaries of the climate than the present energy sources. For instance, solar power is degraded on cloudy days, hydro power suffers when there are droughts, and wind power depends on good winds. Furthermore, these are not independent weather factors. For example, the period of drought on the West Coast in 1976–1977 and

1977–1978 was also a period of generally weak winds, since both were determined by a more or less stationary "blocking pattern" in the pressure field. Clearly, climate variability and change should be taken into account when planning for such renewable energy resources.

Another major potential source of energy is the biomass, which is largely concentrated in the tropics. According to Lieth (1973):

Biological productivity is limited by availability of nutrients and lack of soil moisture, but given adequate soil and rainfall it tends to double for every 10°C increase in mean annual temperature between –10°C and 20°C.

The tropical forests provide wood fuel for some 2 billion people in developing countries (McKay and Allsopp, 1980), and its popularity is increasing in areas like New England and the Rocky Mountains as fossil fuels become more expensive.

It might appear that areas of biomass production would extend poleward as the climate warms from carbon dioxide. But, as was pointed out in Chapter II, the warming will be accompanied by shifts of rainfall as well as temperature patterns. Furthermore the soils of the Arctic North America and Asia are relatively poor in nutrients. These conditions may not support an increased biomass even if temperatures increase. Thus, it is not obvious that climate change alone will increase biomass as an energy source. However, agricultural and forest management practices may improve the situation, regardless of any climate change.

To summarize, energy demands and supplies are both affected by climate variability. But if we plan properly for the vagaries of climate we can withstand year to year climate changes. As discussed in Section 1, this increased flexibility should also help to mitigate the effects of a more gradual climate change.

A global warming will ease the requirements for space heating in temperate latitudes in winter but increase requirements for cooling, shifting the demand from the direct use of fuel to electricity. The patterns of energy use will not move uniformly poleward; there will be marked regional differences in the temperature and precipitation changes due to altered positions of the large scale features of the atmospheric circulation. When our climate scenarios have been refined somewhat the net effects on energy demand could be estimated, since the relationships between energy used and seasonal "degree days" have been reasonably well established. However, in such a study the move to renewable energy resources, especially solar heating, would have to be taken into account.

## 3. World Food Production

The stability and distribution of food production could be greatly affected by a large scale climatic warming. Plant physiology, pests, water availability, and soil conditions are vital to crop growth and are likely to be altered if global temperatures increased.

We can look to a warmer period in the past to see how complex the patterns of change can be. During the Altithermal Period (which we mentioned briefly in Chapter II), some 4500 to 8000 years ago, much of northern and eastern Africa were wetter than now. People lived and probably grazed their cattle in many parts of what is now the Sahara Desert, and the present "corn belt" of the U.S. was generally a dry prairie (see maps of Altithermal Period in Appendix C). Apparently there was not enough summer rainfall to support the forests that thrived later on. Though our map should not be considered a forecast of what might occur if the Earth warms up again, the Altithermal warming, while not caused by carbon dioxide, can nevertheless give us an indication of what *might* happen in the event of a carbon dioxide–induced warming.

Figure III.2 relates world food production to possible changes in soil moisture. This figure combines the data of a few major crops produced in 1978 with a scenario of possible soil moisture patterns for the world (see Figure II.3). For example, the U.S. accounted for nearly half of the world production of maize (corn) in 1978. But according to this scenario, a large portion of its current production areas may become drier in the future.

Experts of the National Academy of Sciences (NAS) consider that "agroclimatic" zones are likely to shift poleward (NAS, 1977b). This would, of course, force farmers to adjust their agricultural practices, but this may not be detrimental.

Provided there is adequate rainfall and suitable soil conditions, longer growing seasons at high temperate latitudes may open lands that are now marginal for growing crops. The northward movement of monsoon rains into the subtropical regions of the world is strongly influenced by the presence of unusual warmth in the Northern Hemisphere. This northward penetration of the monsoon could be enhanced, which in turn may improve agricultural conditions in these areas.

The agricultural productivity of subarctic regions like northern Russia, Canada, and Scandinavia might also be improved by a global

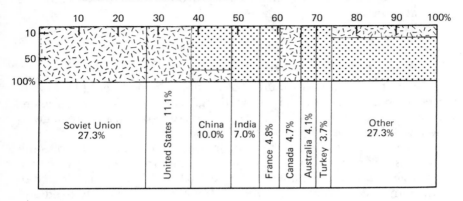

WHEAT 1978 WORLD PRODUCTION — 441474 Thousand Metric Tons

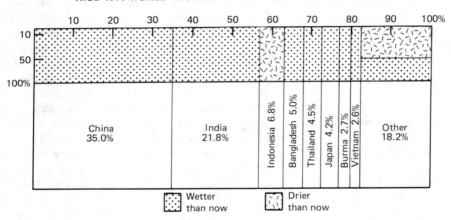

RICE 1978 WORLD PRODUCTION — 376448 Thousand Metric Tons

Wetter than now          Drier than now

**Figure III.2. World food production for some major crops in 1978 combined with a scenario of possible soil moisture patterns on a warmer Earth. Areas marked "Drier than now" and "Wetter than now" are derived from Figure II.3. World food production data compiled from FAO (1979).**

warming. Temperature increases in areas like these that are close to the poles may be about twice the global average increase. Generally, a 1°C increase of mean summertime temperatures can result in an average 10-day increase in the length of the growing season. But as Bollman and Hellyer (1974) have shown, this depends on seasonal durations. For example, an 80-day freeze free period may be altered as much as 20 days

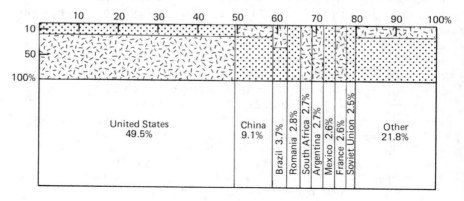

MAIZE (Corn) 1978 WORLD PRODUCTION — 362971 Thousand Metric Tons

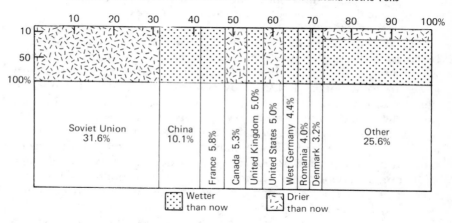

BARLEY 1978 WORLD PRODUCTION — 196123 Thousand Metric Tons

**Figure III.2. (Continued)**

by a 1°C temperature change, while a 120 to 130 day season may only change 6 days (CIAP, 1975).

We should note that every crop responds to climatic factors differently; effects must be examined individually (Thompson, 1975; Bach, 1978). For instance, Biggs and Bartholic (1973) estimate that a 1°C increase in temperature leads to a 2 percent reduction in U.S. corn yield. Ramirez et al. (1975) show that under generally warmer and wetter conditions wheat yields in Illinois and Indiana will be reduced, whereas wheat yields in the major producing states of Kansas, Oklahoma, North Dakota, and South Dakota will increase slightly. Such changes in yield may have significant impacts on the U.S. food system. We need similar estimates for other regions.

Equally important to food production may be the changing climate's effects on the frequency and severity of pest outbreaks. Currently, losses in agriculture and forestry due to pests are extremely high: roughly 37 percent for agriculture and 25 percent for forestry (Dasman, 1972; Pimental et al., 1978). As Pimentel et al., (1978) describe the problem:

> Insect pest populations will generally increase with an increase in temperature. Some insect pests, for example, produce 500 to 2000 offspring per female and go through a generation in 2 to 4 weeks. With a warmer and longer growing season these pests may pass through an additional 1 to 3 generations. The exponential increase of some insect pest populations under the new favorable environment could seriously increase insect losses and make their control more difficult.

Of the world's major crops, pests cause the greatest crop losses in bananas, potatoes, cassava, tomatoes, peanuts, soybeans, millet, maize, wheat and paddy rice (Cramer, 1967). Relating pest–caused world crop losses to food needs, a NAS study (1977b) calculated that if only 20 percent of the current losses in rice production could be prevented, nearly 180 million more people could have a sufficient diet.

With a global warming we can also expect changes in the frequency and geographical distribution of plant disease epidemics. Most current crop production models do not consider the occurrence of plant disease a function of varying climate factors. For instance, scientists are just now recognizing the role of changing climatic conditions in the occurrence of wheat diseases. The severity of stripe rust on winter wheat in the Pacific Northwest has increased since 1961 as a result of higher winter temperatures (Coakley, 1979). It is important to expand the studies of climatic effects on plant disease in order to reduce losses should the expected global surface warming occur.

In addition, collective measures are required if nations are to respond to the threat of losing important plant species. Our present reliance on a limited number of crop species and a narrow genetic base within each of these species is an immediate problem for developed as well as developing countries. According to Mooney (1979):

> Ninety–five percent of human nutrition is derived from no more than 30 plants, eight of which comprise three–quarters of the plant kingdom's contribution to human energy. Three crops — wheat, rice and maize — account for over 75

percent of our cereal consumption. This is not as it has always been. Prehistoric peoples found food in over 1,500 species of wild plants, and at least 500 major vegetables were used in ancient cultivation. In the space of a thousand years, our vegetable food diversity has narrowed to the 200 species grown by backyard gardeners and the 80 species favored by market gardeners. Only 20 vegetable species are used in field cultivation. Modern agricultural history is, at least in part, a history of declining food variety, as more and more people are nourished by fewer and fewer of the world's plant species.

Table III.1 illustrates the restricted genetic base of major U.S. crop varieties. The NAS concluded in its 1972 report that these crops were "impressively uniform genetically and impressively vulnerable."

**Table III.1.** **Some major U.S. crops and the extent to which they are dominated by a few varieties (Myers, 1979).**

|  | Hectares (millions) 1976 | Value ($ millions) 1976 | Total varieties | Major varieties | Hectarage, % of major varieties |
|---|---|---|---|---|---|
| Corn | 33,664 | 14,742 | 197 | 6 | 71 |
| Wheat | 28,662 | 6,201 | 269 | 10 | 55 |
| Soybean | 20,009 | 8,487 | 62 | 6 | 56 |
| Cotton | 4,411 | 3,350 | 50 | 3 | 53 |
| Rice | 1,012 | 770 | 14 | 4 | 65 |
| Potato | 556 | 1,182 | 82 | 4 | 72 |
| Peanut | 611 | 749 | 15 | 9 | 95 |
| Peas | 51 | 22 | 50 | 2 | 96 |

Our narrow crop genetic base can be highly vulnerable to climatic variations, pests, and pathogens. Myers (1979) gives a particularly striking example of this. Here, he points out, is what can happen if we rely on "miracle strains" of the Green Revolution: A type of rice in the Philippines, IR–8, was hit by tungro virus. So rice growers switched to IR–20, a hybrid that proved vulnerable to grassy stunt virus and brown hopper insects. Farmers then tried IR–26, a "superhybrid" that turned out to be resistant to almost all Philippine diseases and insect pests. But IR–26 was too fragile for the islands' strong winds, so plant breeders decided to try a Taiwan strain that could withstand the winds. But IR–26 had been eliminated by Taiwan farmers — they were planting virtually all their ricelands with IR–8. Hence, we can see that expanding genetic diversity in current crop species will offer a measure of protection against potential climate changes.

Multinational corporate control over specific crops should also be considered. Commenting on the accelerating pace of new corporate giants into the seed industry, Mooney (1979) notes:

> Seed corn in the U.S.A., for instance, is by far the most important seed commodity, but roughly two-thirds of all sales flow to only four companies: Dekalb, Pioneer, Sandoz, and Ciba-Geigy . . . The global leader, however, appears to be Royal Dutch/Shell — the petroleum and chemical company headquartered in London and Amsterdam. This firm controls the destiny of thirty seed companies in Europe and North America.

These corporations, among others, could strongly affect the rapidly decreasing stocks of wild strains and disease-resistant varieties of crops for food production. There are widely differing views as to how international regulation of the environmental and economic policies of the multinational corporations could be administered, and what the political effects would be (Vernon, 1968; Kernan, 1970; Nelson, 1970; Falk, 1971; Coan et al., 1974). However, their role in this problem, and potential international genetic resource safeguards, deserve investigation.

We may find that an increase in carbon dioxide could in some respects turn out to be a useful resource for crop production. Summarized below are some of the ways in which yield, quality, and photosynthetic rates can be enhanced. It is known that increased carbon dioxide can, for many plant species (DOE, 1979):

- increase average net photosynthesis;
- change leaf area and leaf structure;
- change canopy shape;
- change the pattern of photosynthetic allocation;
- increase water use efficiency;
- increase tolerance to toxic atmospheric gases;
- change root/shoot ratios;
- change flowering dates and increase number of flowers produced per individual;
- increase number and size of fruits and number of seeds produced per plant;
- affect germination of some species.

Allen (1979) demonstrated that greenhouse grown vegetable crops with added carbon dioxide have increased yields by at least 20 percent. And Wittwer (1980) points out that:

> Yield responses peak at 1000 to 1200 ppmv [parts per million by volume] of atmospheric carbon dioxide . . . [This is over 3 times the preindustrial level.] The potential for increased

photosynthesis is about 0.5 percent for each one percent
increase in the concentration of atmospheric carbon dioxide
in the range of 100 to 300 ppmv above ambient.

These results might lead us to conclude that elevated levels of
atmospheric carbon dioxide could, of itself, have very beneficial effects
on world food production. However, at this stage we are unable to
determine whether these beneficial effects on plant growth will be offset
by other climate and environmental responses. As a 1976 NAS study
notes:

> Photosynthesis must run effectively if high yields are to be
> obtained. Drought, cool temperatures, flooded soils, or lack
> of nutrients often affect yield by reducing photosynthesis. It
> is important that we not lose sight of these other factors
> associated with the projected climate change and world
> food production.

## 4. Global Ecology

Agriculture for food and fiber production differs from the less
managed ecosystems of the world, such as grasslands, savannas, forests,
tundra, alpine lands, and deserts. While agricultural systems usually
depend on a few specialized plant species, a natural ecosystem, or
biome, represents a diversity of plants and animals that interact and live
in a natural balance — that is, until the balance is disturbed by humans or
by climate change.

Mankind has already significantly influenced many biomes. Forests
are managed for their wood products (Baumgartner, 1979), rangelands
are grazed by cattle and thus modified (VanDyne and Pendleton, 1980),
and semi-deserts are formed where overgrazing or bad agricultural
practices have caused vegetation and top soil to disappear
(Oguntoyinbo and Odingo, 1979).

There are few, if any, ecosystems remaining in the world that are free
from human influence. Among the biomes still close to their natural
states are the tropical forests that have not yet been exploited and the
unpopulated tundra areas in the Arctic. However, both are likely to
experience changes in the near future due to human-induced climate
shifts. We will discuss this in more detail later in this section.

When human activities in a region cease, the natural ecological
conditions can be restored fairly quickly. But when climatic change
affects a biome on a longer time scale, the effects are considerably more
dramatic and permanent (Gerasimov, 1979; Lamb, 1977; Wijmstra, 1979).
If a change of either mean temperature or annual precipitation (see
Figure III.3) occurs in a given region, conditions will probably become

71

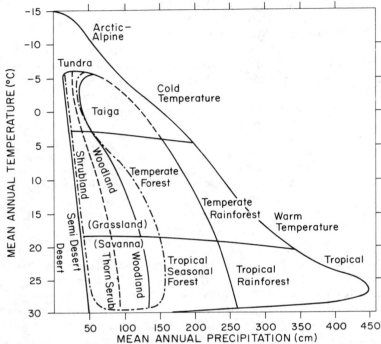

**Figure III.3.** World biome types as they are determined by precipitation and temperature. The boundaries between types are approximate. The dot–dash line encloses a wide range of environments in which either grassland or one of the types dominated by woody plants may form the prevailing vegetation (Whittaker, 1975).

less favorable and the biome will be modified. Bolin (1979) has emphasized the importance of the rate of change of a biome due to some external influence such as shifts in climate:

- *Instantaneous ecosystem response.* The rate at which an ecosystem takes up nutrients and gives off carbon dioxide depends in part on its leaf area and canopy structures. The characteristics of its environment such as temperature, soil moisture, solar radiation, nutrient content of the soil, and carbon dioxide in the atmosphere are also important. According to Bolin (1979), the tools are available to compute how biomes will react to a suddenly altered climate.

- *Intermediate ecosystem response.* If abnormal climate prevails for some years or decades, a biome may be able to adjust to the new environmental conditions by modifying its "climax" structure, thereby approaching a new equilibrium.

● *Long term ecosystem response.* If a marked climatic change takes place and lasts for a century or more (which is considerably longer than the life span of most species in the biome) a succession to a new biome may be initiated. This would be most likely to occur where a neighboring biome is well adapted to the new conditions; the region's position on Figure III.3 would then shift.

Climate change due to increasing carbon dioxide will take place on the intermediate time scale referred to here. But ultimately the new climate regime will probably last for many centuries, causing long term ecosystem responses. We have seen examples of the latter in the climate record of the past several thousand years. For example, Nichols (1975) reports that 3000 to 4000 years ago in north–central Canada the Arctic tundra migrated 300 to 400 kilometers into an area once covered by spruce trees. The likely cause was a combination of increasingly cold climate and more frequent forest fires due to a general drying of the region. Another example, already cited in Chapter II, is the transition of a dry grassland that sustained wild animals, and perhaps herds of cattle, to what is now the Sahara Desert. This change seems to have occurred rather rapidly around 5000 years ago (Flohn and Nicholson, 1980; Lamb, 1977), although there is evidence suggesting that a temporary return to a moister regime may have occured around 4000 years ago.

Earlier we mentioned climate changes in the tropics and Arctic tundra, the two biomes still close to their natural states. Shifts in precipitation patterns or temperature will mean significant changes for both of these biomes.

Forests, for instance, require relatively high precipitation (Baumgartner, 1979). They consume more water than other kinds of vegetation, and transfer it back to the air through their leaves by a process called evapotranspiration. In semiarid areas, where water is precious, trees are extremely susceptible to small decreases in precipitation; in wet areas where forests thrive, they reduce soil erosion and minimize the loss of nutrients. Many kinds of trees are vulnerable to insect pests, and infestations are markedly influenced by temperature and precipitation. Hence, these factors suggest that climatic change, especially changes in precipitation, will have a significant effect on the distribution of areas favorable for forests.

For the frozen tundra of the Arctic Basin a warming induced by increased carbon dioxide would also have a very large influence. This biome is characterized by permafrost, which accounts for its low–growing vegetation, lack of trees, and poor drainage in summer. This last characteristic causes swamps, small ponds, and lakes to form, and deep deposits of organic matter, referred to as peat, to accumulate. While peat accumulation rates in tropical or temperate areas may be greater than in the Arctic, the fact that the organic matter remains saturated with water in summer and frozen the rest of the year prevents it from oxidizing and decaying (Bolin, 1979; TIE, 1980).

If a warming trend occurred in the tundra the permafrost would retreat, allowing trees to grow further poleward, as occurred during the Altithermal Period in Canada (Nichols, 1975). The upper layers of peat would dry out, allowing oxidation and decay to take place, and this would release carbon dioxide into the atmosphere. The extra carbon dioxide would enhance the warming, creating a positive feedback (see Section II.2).

In summary, the distribution of the various biomes of the world depends primarily on climate, in particular mean temperature and precipitation, as shown in Figure III.3. Other factors are likely to be involved as well, such as soil type and the seasonal variations of soil moisture. After a carbon dioxide-induced climate change has occurred, conditions favorable for a biome may no longer exist in its current location. The response of each ecosystem will be to seek a new equilibrium and to gradually invade neighboring areas where the new climate is more favorable. These shifts of biomes may be predictable for a given scenario of regional and seasonal climate change, assuming that natural processes alone will be involved. However, in many parts of the world human intervention will probably have a larger ecological impact than the climate in the next 50 to 100 years.

## 5. Water Resources

Water is fundamental to agriculture, industry, plant and animal life. It has been an important economic resource and political tool since the beginning of human history. An insightful study by Wittfogel (1957) underscores the special role water control methods have played, especially in water-deficient lands. Wittfogel notes that:

> Of all tasks imposed by the natural environment, it was the
> task imposed by a precarious water situation that stimulated
> man to develop hydraulic [i.e., large-scale, government-
> directed irrigation and farming] methods of social control.

Carbon dioxide-induced global climatic changes, when they occur, could affect water supply and distribution, perhaps adversely for some (see Section II.4). The hydrologic cycle is an important component of the climate system and determines regional water availability: precipitation and soil moisture storage add to the water supply, while evaporation, transpiration, and runoff subtract from it.

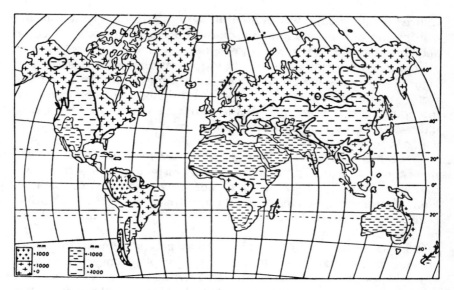

**Figure III.4. Water-deficiency (–) and water-surplus (+) zones in the world. A water deficiency exists if precipitation supplies less water than would be needed for well watered vegetation. In the reverse circumstances there is a water surplus (Falkenmark and Lindh, 1976).**

If the total annual precipitation were evenly distributed, every region in the world would receive about 86 centimeters (More, 1967). But as it is, annual distributions range from under 25 centimeters to more than 254 centimeters. According to Oliver (1973): "In terms of management of water resources by man, it is the areas of scant or excessive precipitation that merit the most attention."

Areas of the world in which there is currently a water surplus or a water deficiency are illustrated in Figure III.4. It is apparent from the map that on the whole populations of developing countries experience greater water deficiencies than populations of developed countries. Climatic extremes, scarcity of land, and the lack of capital investment in water resource developments make developing countries particularly vulnerable to changes in water supply.

Changes in precipitation due to an atmospheric warming represent a key element in the study of potential climatic impacts on water supplies, and hence food. Precipitation is, after all, the prime source of all our fresh water. Water resource planning for a markedly different future climate regime will depend in large part upon changes in the distribution of precipitation and soil moisture over time and space. In Sections II.3 and II.4 it was shown that we should expect marked alterations in the global precipitation patterns on a warmer earth, and Figure II.3 represents a possible scenario of where conditions might be wetter or drier than the present. We must stress again that this map is not intended to be a prediction of the future climate, but rather a vivid illustration of the kinds of changes that may occur in the availability of water in some regions.

In terms of food production, a part of the CIAP (1975) study showed that changes in overall production caused by a temperature increase will be relatively small if there is no accompanying change in precipitation. Hence, the changes in precipitation that result from a global temperature increase have a greater effect on food production than a temperature increase alone.

Similarly, for forest and range land, precipitation is the major climatic factor that determines the type of plant cover in an area, although locally the quality of soil can override the climatic effects (see Section 4). The changes in the overall production of a natural ecosystem caused by an increase in temperature will be relatively small if there is no change in precipitation. The CIAP (1975) study showed almost a "... straight line inverse relation between average annual precipitation and acres of native perennial grassland (range) required on average per mature cow for six months of summer grazing, seemingly irrespective of temperature or evaporation" (see Figure III.5). The U.S. Department of Agriculture (USDA) Soil Conservation Service (1964) found an 800 pound (air dried) per acre increase in rangeland production for every 5 inch increase in average annual precipitation across the northern plains. Here again, the changes in precipitation that result from an increase in temperature will have a much greater effect on the ability of natural ecosystems to produce than the increase in temperature itself.

The effect of climatic change on water resources has been sketched by Schwartz (1977). His speculations on the effects of climatic change in the northwestern U.S. are illustrated in Table III.2. Note that the effect of an increase in the *variance* of streamflow is likely to be more severe than a decrease in the *mean* flow, a recurrent theme in assessing the nature of any climatic change.

As an example of long range planning to reduce vulnerability to climatic fluctuations, the Soviet Union has initiated several elaborate schemes designed to bring a new water supply to agricultural land. According to Roberts (1980):

Perhaps the most ambitious plan ever conceived for

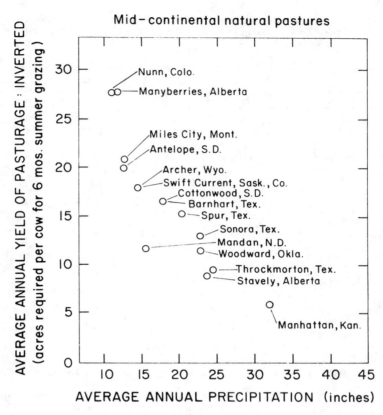

**Figure III.5. Data on grazing trails throughout the U.S. and Canada showing acres required per cow vs. average annual precipitation (CIAP, 1975).**

irrigation to contend both with a normally arid climate and a fluctuating water supply is that of the Soviet Union for the vast desert in the Kazakhstan and Uzbekistan. This vast region, stretching for about 1500 kilometers east of the Caspian Sea and embracing the drainage basin for the Aral Sea, has great potential for agricultural development if well irrigated. To the north, across the divide to the Arctic Sea, lie the large rivers Ob and Yenisei, whose waters flow abundantly and unexploited to the Arctic. The monumental project calls for diversion of a major fraction of the Ob River flow southwards to the desert.

The plan is a three-stage project designed to divert to the desert one-half of the river's 400 cubic kilometers per

**Table III.2.** Criteria of water supply systems and possible effects of climatic change. These possibilities pertain especially to the northeast United States (Adapted from Schwartz, 1977).

| Attributes of Water Supply Systems | Parameters of Climatic Change | |
|---|---|---|
| | Decrease in Mean Streamflow | Increase in Variance of Streamflow |
| 1. Yield from unregulated streams | Some effects, generally small if change in mean is small | Severe effects; usually short term |
| 2. Yield from reservoirs | Significant to severe effects particularly if reservoirs develop a high percentage of the average flow | Medium to no effects depending on reservoir size in relation to drainage area; larger reservoirs will suffer smaller effects |
| 3. Yield from groundwater | Significant in the long run | Little if any significance |
| 4. Quality of raw water | Probably insignificant effects except where large reservoirs are drawn to low levels | Generally no effects except possible increase in turbidity during high flows |
| 5. System reliability | Some effects, other than those in 1–4 | Some reduction in addition to effects under 1–4 |
| 6. Effectiveness of inter-system and interbasin connections | No change | Increased effectiveness if variance increases |
| 7. Magnitude and control of demand | No significant effect | No significant effect |
| 8. Cost of operation of water system | No significant effects; new construction might eventually alleviate long term shortages | Possible increase due to turbidity, increased pumping between systems if applicable |
| 9. Pressure on and ability of the water system to respond to change | Pressure to expand if shortages occur repeatedly; ability to respond would not be affected by hydrologic events | Pressure to expand but rapid return to normal may inhibit expansion |

year flow through a series of tunnels, canals and pumping stations 2500 kilometers long. Scheduled for completion by the year 2000 . . . the project will reduce the vulnerability to climate fluctuations of Soviet grain production.

In sum, measures taken now to guarantee more reliable water supply would be advantageous regardless of longer term climatic changes. Such measures would include improving existing dams and irrigation facilities and creating new ones, both for cultivated acreage and for areas where there is potential for expanding the productivity of land. Guaranteeing more regular water supply and optimum production of water resources will help raise total world food output and make agricultural production less susceptible to both short term climatic fluctuations and long term climatic change.

## 6. Fisheries

From the 1950s to early 1970s rivers, lakes, and coastal areas were viewed as vast almost limitless resources that could meet increased world demands for protein. Scientists reported that fish catches in the late 1960s and early 1970s would supply huge increases (Mosaic, 1975), and would supplement food production on land. Fish as a direct human food source was thought to be increasingly important as the world population was becoming dependent on only about thirty plant and six animal species (see Section 3).

But then the relative stability of fish supply was threatened, dampening that optimism: In 1972 there were sharp declines in catches of Peruvian anchovies, South African pilchards, Atlanto–Scandian herrings, and the California sardines (Cram, 1980; Swaminathan, 1979; Radovich, 1980).

While the economic value of the world's fisheries has partially recovered in the past few years, the level of commercial fish production on a global scale has remained appreciably below 1971 production levels. For example, the total catches reached a peak of 26.5 million tons in 1970; by 1973 the hauls had declined to 18.5 million tons (FAO, 1978). The projections shown in Table III.3 indicate that the near future rate of increase in the world catch of fish is unlikely to lead to catches exceeding the period of 1974. By 1985 developed countries' catches are expected to show little change from those of 1972 to 1974. Prospects appear better for developing countries.

The decline in fish catch since 1972 raises serious questions about the sea as a reliable food source (Brown with Eckholm, 1974). It also arouses heightened concern about the climatic variables associated with fishery food chain dynamics (Cushing, 1979). Belatedly, we are realizing just how fragile fish populations can be, because of the variability of climate and other environmental factors, mismanagement of fish resources, or some combination of both (Glantz, 1979; Cram, 1980). For instance, the Peruvian anchovy decline might have been largely due to mismanagement practices that led to overfishing (Clark, 1977; Brown with Eckholm, 1974).

As Hjul (1977) noted:

One of the acute problems of the fishery scientist trying to

**Table III.3.** Rate of growth of world fisheries production: past and future. The total growth rates were computed from unrounded data and exclude whales. The "basic" projections assume a continuation of the presently depressed condition of the anchoveta fishery in Peru and northern Chile, whereas the "supplementary" projections assume a recovery of the anchoveta fishery to an annual production of 7 million tons (Adapted from FAO, 1978).

| | Growth Rates | | |
|---|---|---|---|
| | Actual 1962-64 to 1972-74 | Projected 1972-74 to 1985 | |
| | | Basic | Supplementary |
| WORLD TOTALS | 3.5 | 1.1 | 2.0 |
| DEVELOPING COUNTRY TOTALS | 2.9 | 2.0 | 3.6 |
| Latin America | –3.3 | 1.5 | 6.5 |
| Africa | 7.6 | 1.9 | 3.1 |
| Near East | 4.3 | 3.7 | 4.4 |
| Far East | 6.5 | 2.4 | 2.9 |
| Asian Centrally Planned Economies | 4.7 | 1.8 | 1.8 |
| Other Developing Countries | 12.4 | 4.7 | 6.4 |
| DEVELOPED COUNTRY TOTALS | 4.0 | 0.3 | 0.5 |
| North America | –0.4 | 2.9 | 3.9 |
| Western Europe | 2.8 | 0.4 | 0.5 |
| European Economic Community | 2.3 | 0.1 | 0.2 |
| Other Western Europe | 3.2 | 0.7 | 0.7 |
| Eastern Europe and U.S.S.R. | 8.0 | 0.0 | 0.0 |
| Eastern Europe | 9.5 | –0.5 | –0.5 |
| Oceania | 5.5 | 6.0 | 7.3 |
| Other Developed Countries | 4.4 | –0.8 | –0.7 |
| | ( . . . percent per annum . . . ) | | |

keep a protective watch on a resource being fished is that conclusive evidence of overfishing comes when the damage has been done and is then too late.

But our primary concern here is with the climatic effects on fish yields. There are several examples of how a change in temperature (combined with other factors) can alter the size of catches.

Cushing (1979) studied the long term effects of increased temperatures on the abundance of the West Greenland cod fishery. He noted that:

During the late nineteenth century no cod were caught on the offshore banks during various exploratory voyages. On the Tjalfe expedition in 1908–10 a few were found there, and in 1912 24 tons were taken ... The stock was established off West Greenland with a series of strong year classes, 1917, 1922, 1926, 1934 and 1936, and by the thirties annual catches had built up to 70,000 tons ... Later year classes, 1945 and 1949, increased the stock again until catches in the fifties and early sixties reached as much as 450,000 tons. The last good year class appeared in 1963 and the last significant one in 1968; in recent years, catches have been banned off Greenland.

Up to about 1950 a rise in North Atlantic temperatures may have improved the West Greenland cod catch, and subsequent temperature decreases may have contributed to the decline.

Another example of climatic influences on fisheries is that of the Peruvian anchovies. In 1972 the coastal waters around Peru increased several degrees above normal, and as a result, anchovies either dispersed, failed to spawn, or died. The coastal warming was associated with a phenomenon called El Niño, which is a temporary decrease in the upwelling process that is vitally important to the marine food chain. Stidd (1976) explains:

Along the shore, cool water has to come up from the bottom to replace the surface water drifting seaward ... As marine organisms die and sink they leave the upper layers where sunlight is still available to promote growth. They collect in the darkness of the ocean bottom and decompose. Along the west coasts of continents the upwelling brings the resulting nutrients back to the surface where sunlight and oxygen can promote growth. The nutrients enter the food chain going from phytoplankton to zooplankton to larvae to fish.

Peru's anchovy catch plummeted from a record high of 12.5 million metric tons in 1970 to less than 2 million metric tons in 1973. After a brief increase in the mid-1970s it declined even further to about 1 million metric tons in 1979 (Glantz, 1979). From 1970 to 1973 the economic value of Peru's catch dropped from $187.2 million to $85.9 million (Bell, 1978). This dramatic decline in turn affected the Peruvian fishmeal industry and, recently, the world price of fishmeal, soybean, and other feed grains (Stidd, 1976; Vondruska, 1980).

The Peruvian coastal region is just one of several major coastal zones dependent on the biological productivity that occurs from upwelling (Ryther, 1969; Cushing, 1975). In addition to Peru, upwelling regions exist off the coasts of California, Namibia, Somalia, and Mauritania, and these contributed almost half of the world's fish supply in the early 1970s.

Other examples of temperature fluctuations affecting fish categories are the following:

- Appolonio and Dunton (1969) reported that high temperatures might be directly linked to the collapse of the northern U.S. shrimp industry in the mid–1950s;
- Anthony and Clark (1978) also investigated this industry and the detrimental effect that increased sea water temperatures may have had between 1968 and 1975;
- Houghton (1980) has shown that the growth rates of cod stocks in the North Atlantic are apparently affected by a fluctuation of sea temperatures.

Fishery managers are aware of how temperature fluctuations can influence their stock. But we should point out that understanding the reasons for fluctuation in fish productivity requires more than just studying temperature changes. Other climatic variables and associated oceanic conditions such as prevailing winds and ocean currents, cloud cover, rainfall patterns, and availability of nutrients are also linked with fish breeding and survival. It is important that we know more about these variables and how they affect fish population dynamics and consequently fishery yields.

## 7. Health, Comfort, and Disease

Climates of the world where populations can live and flourish fall within a temperature range known as the "comfort zone." The limits of thermal tolerance for human beings extends between an upper limit of 50°C and a lower limit of –60°C. Figure III.6 illustrates climatic zones where most of the world's population lives.

Several "comfort indices" have been set up as methods to determine the effects of high or low temperatures or other stresses on individuals' physiological, intellectual, and social functioning (Vernon, 1932; Belding and Hatch, 1955; Consolazio et al., 1963; Griffitt, 1970; McKerslake, 1972; Weihe, 1979). These studies lend support to the common belief that very high or very low temperatures can negatively influence many personal functions and social behaviors. They also serve as a starting point for projecting some of the behavioral and health impacts of a future global surface warming.

The capacity for physical performance and personal motivation depend in part on prevailing climatic conditions. This pertains to work patterns as well as to certain types of sport activities (Rohles, 1970; Parsons, 1979; Weihe, 1979). In studies of the effects of temperature on

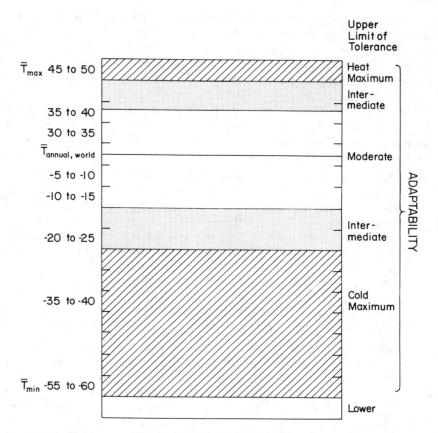

**Figure III.6.** Human population – climate interaction. White zone: range of minimum and maximum temperature bands where over 60 percent of the world's population lives, requiring moderate adaptability. Dotted zone: range where about 30 percent of the world's population lives, requiring intermediate adaptability. Hatched zone: range where less than 10 percent of the world's population lives, requiring maximum adaptability near the limits of tolerance (Weihe, 1979).

Western workers, for example, it has been reported (Harrison, 1979) that:

> A loss of output of 2 percent to 4 percent [occurs] for every rise in temperature of one degree centigrade. Thus a 10°C temperature difference between a tropical and a temperate country might reduce labor productivity in the former by 20 percent to 40 percent, or more when humidity is high.

Disease constitutes another very important factor that should be studied in the context of a potential carbon dioxide–induced climatic change. Altered climatic patterns, including increasing precipitation and ground water, and seasonal temperature extremes could critically affect breeding conditions, growth rates, and biological diversity of many species including parasites affecting humans.

To illustrate the possible consequences of a global climatic warming on the incidence of specific diseases in different regions, we examine below a few diseases that are of considerable socioeconomic significance in the countries where they are prevalent.

- **Schistosomiasis.** Found largely in countries with warm climates and particularly in rural tropical and subtropical areas (see Fig. III.7). Schistosomiasis affects over 200 million people, and its prevalence is increasing (Rée, 1977). The ova of the Schistoma parasite penetrate the skin of vertebrate hosts. Large human populations using a small water supply, especially artificial reservoirs, run increased risks of infection. In humans, the colon, liver and bladder are affected by this disease. It also tends to deplete a person's energy and causes a high death rate, especially among infants. The range of this parasite is confined to regions with mean temperatures between 10° and 37°C (Weihe, 1979).

- **Bacillary dysentery.** This disease may occur anywhere in the world, although it is common in Africa, particularly Mauritania and Chad. The disease tends to be more extensive in the tropics, but epidemics have appeared in temperate regions. According to the World Health Organization (WHO), in 1977 there were 112,366 reported cases of bacillary dysentery in Iran, 26,581 in Czechoslovakia, and 16,584 in the United States. The pathogens are usually transmitted to people by flies. Temperature plays an important role in the spread of the disease: at 16°C it takes a housefly 44 days to develop from an egg into an adult. The hatching time drops dramatically, however, to 16 days when temperature increases to 25°C and to only 10 days when temperature rises to 30°C (May, 1958).

- **Hookworm.** The 1963 African Conference on Ancyclostomiasis (a genus of hookworms) estimated that one-fourth of the world's population is infected by these intestinal helminthiases (CCTA/WHO, 1963). Kamarck (1976) estimates that some 500 million people in the tropical and subtropical regions suffer from hookworm disease, which causes anemia, apathy, and in children mental and physical retardation. The National Academy of

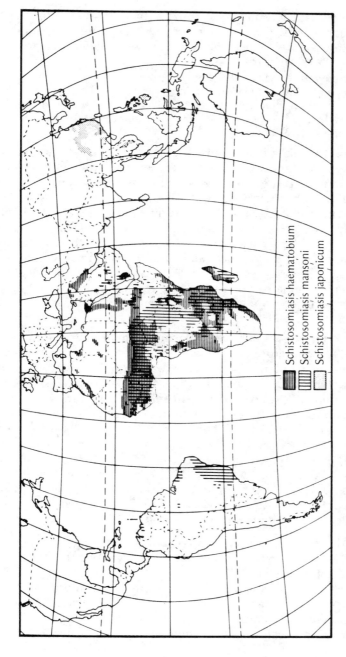

Figure III.7. World distribution of major types of Schistosomiasis. The map illustrates that Schistosomiasis is found largely in tropical and subtropical countries (Ree, 1977).

Schistosomiasis haematobium
Schistosomiasis mansoni
Schistosomiasis japonicum

Sciences (1962) reports that hookworm infestation reduced labor efficiency in parts of Syria by roughly 50 percent. The importance of temperature in the ecology of hookworm larva development is pointed out by Carr (1949):

> Temperature and soil moisture are the two important climatic factors which determine whether the hookworm larva will be able to develop in the soil... The optimum atmospheric temperature for the development of the larva in the soil lies between 25°C and 30°C.

- **Yaws.** Yaws is a contagious disease characterized by bone and joint lesions and which sometimes results in the enlargement of lymph nodes. The disease was a considerable problem in Haiti in 1950, afflicting over 60 percent of the rural population (May, 1958). The disease is commonly found in Panama, Brazil, Colombia, Philippines, Thailand, where its prevalence makes it a public health problem. Approximately 80 percent of the yaws areas are distributed in the tropical and subtropical regions where mean annual temperatures are over 27°C. One notable feature of yaws is that it is climate dependent: the patient can be healed simply by moving away from a hot and humid environment to cooler regions (May, 1958).

- **Other diseases.** There are, of course, many other diseases on which temperature and precipitation seem to have considerable influence. Cholera outbreaks, for instance, have been correlated with climatic factors including increased temperature, humidity, and rainfall (Rogers, 1928; Russell and Sundaranajan, 1928). Certain forms of tuberculosis have been arrested when patients moved to sunny, hot, and dry climates (May, 1958). It has further been observed that the mosquito vector carrying yellow fever stops breeding when exposed to 15°C to 20°C temperatures (Kamarck, 1976; WHO, 1971; Brown, 1977). Finally, the occurrence of meningococcal meningitis (a cerebrospinal disease) has been closely associated with climatic variations, particularly in the Sahel zone (Weihe, 1979).

Different disease agents are differently affected by environmental conditions as well as by their own life cycle. The effects of a climatic change on each disease is difficult to assess owing to the many different geographical conditions and controls, together with the uncertainties about the expected magnitude and course of the climatic change. Further, foreseeable climatic effects on health and disease due to temperature and precipitation change will vary with the nature and condition of water supplies, dietary and cropping customs, food sanitation, and refuse disposal. In this sense, the complex natural histories of diseases are not solely linked to climate factors, but are also conditioned by the hygienic measures of societies and the amount of investment available for economic growth (DeLancey, 1978; Patterson and Hartwig, 1978). For example, malaria eradication has been achieved in the United States, where almost one-quarter of the population now resides in a previously malarious area (Learmonth, 1977). Not surprisingly, most of the serious disease agents are disproportionately concentrated in the poor and developing countries of the world.

## 8.  Population Settlements

Alterations in human settlement patterns may result from a warming of the Earth's surface and consequent shift of deserts and rainfall patterns, as well as from a changing sea level. Belatedly, some governments and intergovernmental organizations are realizing that climate stresses can have an important impact on urban-rural and international migration patterns.

The recent deaths (estimated at between 100,000 and 200,000) and shift of nomadic populations during the drought of 1968-1973 in the Sahelian nations of Senegal, Mali, Mauritania, Upper Volta, and Chad, has presented us with a tragic example of how climatic stresses can in part affect migration patterns (Campbell, 1977).

The effects of climatic fluctuation on migration are amplified in developing countries by their proximity to the physical and economic margins of regions where growth and development can take place. Regarding Latin American migration trends, Mortara (1967) notes:

> A number of the circumstances contributing to the exodus from rural areas are related to the natural environment. Among the physical factors we may mention climatic and meteorological disasters, which make life difficult for inhabitants of such areas by exposing them to hardships and dangers and by reducing the size of harvests, damaging crops and decimating livestock.

Since about 22 percent of the world population in 2000 is estimated to be in the more developed regions and 78 percent in the less developed regions of the world, the short term effects of climatic fluctuations on populations in the latter zones must be viewed as a central factor in plans and programs dealing with future climate-societal problems (UNFPA, 1979).

Understanding how past populations dealt with climatic fluctuations and changes may be helpful when analyzing current and future impacts. For example, historians provide good evidence that the political strife and eventual dispersal of the ancient Mycenaeans around 1230 B.C. was accompanied by severe droughts and grain shortages (Carpenter, 1966; Bryson and Murray, 1977). The period around 1450 in Europe has been described as widespread *Wustungen* (abandonment of agricultural areas and villages), apparently associated with severe winters and variable summers that ruined crops and pastures (Flohn, 1950; Lamb, 1977). Anxiety about the unpredictable nature of climate led to a debate by the Danish government in 1784 whether ice encroaching on Iceland might require an evacuation of that country (Koch, 1945; Lamb, 1977).

Between 1845 and 1851 a run of warm and moist summers in Ireland helped the potato blight fungus multiply, which has been linked to the so-called "Irish Potato Famine"; the famine nearly halved the Irish population as people emigrated to the United States and to Britain.

Migration was particularly high during the 1890s drought period in the United States. An estimated 300,000 farmers and settlers were displaced, mainly from the high and western plains frontier (Climate and Society Research Group, 1979).

The Dust Bowl in Kansas, Texas, and Oklahoma during the 1930s is a modern analog of short term abandonment of farmland, partly due to abnormal rainfall and temperatures but also due to poorly managed grazing and plowing policies (Parry, 1978). At the same time more than 580,000 people also left the American and Canadian sections of the Great Plains for the West Coast and cities of the East (Beltzner, 1976). Figure III.8. graphically depicts the relevant demographic processes in the United States over the period 1920–1940.

One long term scenario for climatic warming due to increased carbon dioxide depicts the disintegration of the unstable West Antarctic ice sheet (see Section II.3.) that would cause a sea level rise of some 5 to 8 meters. If this ice sheet slipped into the surrounding ocean it would submerge coastlines worldwide and cause acute demographic shifts. There is actually considerable scientific debate on when this would occur and what the time scale would be, whether in a few decades or a few centuries (Bentley, 1980). Schneider and Chen (1980) estimate that should this occur:

> For a 15–foot (5 meters) rise, over 11 million people (about 6 percent of the 1970 continental United States population) . . . are affected; for the 28–foot (8 meters) case, these values increase to about 16 million people (8 percent) . . . On a regional scale, the impacts are yet more severe: some 40 percent of Florida's population . . . are affected in the 15–foot case and an additional 10 to 15 percent . . . in the 25–foot case.

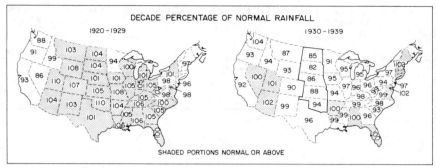

DECADE PERCENTAGE OF NORMAL RAINFALL

1920-1929       1930-1939

SHADED PORTIONS NORMAL OR ABOVE

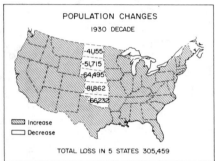

POPULATION CHANGES
1930 DECADE

Increase
Decrease

TOTAL LOSS IN 5 STATES 305,459

**Figure III.8.** **Population shifts and climate changes in the U.S., 1920–1940. A large population drop is evident in North and South Dakota, Nebraska, Kansas, and Oklahoma during the period of below normal rainfall (Tannehill, 1947).**

The dramatic population shifts likely to occur as a result of adjustment to coastal flooding are summarized for the continental United States in Table III.4.

More than 30 percent of the world's population lives within a 50 kilometer area adjoining oceans and seas. In the United States seven of the nine largest metropolitan areas are within the 101,500 mile coastal zone (CEQ, 1979). Venetians well know the effects of "acqua alta" — highwater — on land surface drainage, erosion, existing port facilities, and densely populated river deltas. But this information has received remarkably little attention elsewhere. Less than a handful of studies are available on the demographic and economic impacts of a carbon dioxide–induced rise in sea level (Kellogg, 1978; Schneider and Chen, 1980).

Despite the uncertainties about the future behavior of the West Antarctic ice sheet, there is a great deal we already know about land use, floods and climatic variability to protect societies from related deaths and property losses. Thus, along with detailed examination of the vulnerability of the West Antarctic ice sheet to a carbon dioxide–induced

**Table III.4.** Summary of estimated geographic and demographic impacts of 15- and 25-foot (4.6- and 7.6-meter) rises in sea level for the continental United States (Adapted from Schneider and Chen, 1980)a.

| Region/State | 15-Foot Case | | | 25-Foot Case | | |
|---|---|---|---|---|---|---|
| | % Flooded | Pop. (millions) | Approx. % of State | % Flooded | Pop. (millions) | Approx. % of State |
| Florida | 24.1 | 2.9 | 43 | 35.5 | 3.8 | 55 |
| Gulf Coast | 4.7 | 2.7 | — | 5.8 | 3.3 | — |
| Texas | 2.2 | 0.9 | 8 | 3.2 | 1.3 | 11 |
| Louisiana | 27.5 | 1.7 | 46 | 31.4 | 1.8 | 50 |
| Mississippi | 1.0 | c | 2 | 1.5 | 0.1 | 4 |
| Alabama | 0.8 | c | 2 | 1.1 | 0.1 | 2 |
| Mid-Atlantic | 5.3 | 1.8 | — | 7.6 | 2.5 | — |
| Georgia | 2.4 | 0.2 | 4 | 4.0 | 0.3 | 6 |
| South Carolina | 6.7 | 0.3 | 10 | 10.2 | 0.3 | 13 |
| North Carolina | 7.9 | 0.2 | 3 | 9.8 | 0.2 | 4 |
| Virginia | 3.1 | 0.7 | 16 | 4.8 | 1.0 | 21 |
| Maryland | 12.3 | 0.2 | 6 | 17.3 | 0.4 | 10 |
| Dist. of Col. | 15.0 | 0.1 | 15 | 20.0 | 0.2 | 20 |
| Delaware | 16.0 | 0.1 | 19 | 25.0 | 0.1 | 25 |

a   Totals may not add exactly due to rounding errors.
c   Less than 0.1.

warming and the probability of a subsequent rise in sea level, we should increase the resilience of populated areas less than 5 meters above sea level. The distillation and use of climatological and environmental information in land use planning along shores in this zone could significantly help to prevent or at least mitigate future climatic impacts, and is a measure that would be beneficial for many other reasons.

## 9.   Tourism and Recreation

Climatic conditions in part determine the environment in which recreational activities take place, as well as affecting the demand for and supply of outdoor recreational facilities. Climatic variations are known to influence human performance and physiological behavior, as we saw in Section 7. Hentschel (1964) and Green (1967) emphasize the effects of an increased temperature on individual comfort, which also influences a desire to engage in active sports. Furthermore, it is evident from various studies that climatic conditions have definite effects on seasonal population distributions and vacation choices (Clawson, 1966).

There are many areas of the world that have climates which encourage recreational activities. Indeed, tourism and recreation form an important industry in many places. But the effects of a global atmospheric warming may make some areas more suitable for outdoor recreation and leave others less attractive. For example, decreased snowfall would affect regions that have become popular ski resorts. Increased precipitation in other areas would enhance water-related recreational activities, such as boating and swimming (Paul, 1972; Perry, 1972). But climatic variability can impact the tourists too. It has been shown to affect income distributions and hence the ability of people to afford vacations and recreation (Rohles, 1970; Parsons, 1979).

Services related to tourism and recreation are also likely to be affected. These enterprises include transportation, accommodations, sporting equipment supplies, and insurance services (Hendrick, 1965).

As concern for the general well-being and health of individuals grows throughout the world, outdoor recreation and sports activities programs, tourism, equipment production, and national parks programs can be expected to increase in significance, in both socioeconomic and environmental terms. In meeting this likely increased demand it is clear that a more thorough awareness of the constraints and opportunities of a different climatic regime will be needed.

# REFERENCES

Allen, L.H. 1979: Potentials for carbon dioxide enrichment. In *Modification of the Aerial Environment of Crops*, B.J. Barfield and J.F. Gerber (eds.), Monograph No. 2, American Society of Agricultural Engineers, St. Joseph, Mich., 500–519.

Anthony, V.C. and S. Clark, 1978: A description of the northern shrimp fishery and its decline in relation to water temperature. In *Climate and Fisheries*, Center for Ocean Management Studies, University of Rhode Island, Kingston, RI.

Appolonio, S. and E.E. Dunton, 1969: The northern shrimp in the Gulf of Maine. Comm. Fish. Res. Development Proj. No. 3–12–R.

Bach, W., 1978: The potential consequences of increasing $CO_2$ levels in the atmosphere. In *Carbon Dioxide, Climate and Society*, J. Williams (ed.), Pergamon Press, New York, 141–167.

Baumgartner, A., 1979: Climatic variability and forestry. In *Proceedings of the World Climate Conference*, WMO No. 537, World Meteorological Organization, Geneva, 581–607.

Belding, H.S. and T.F. Hatch, 1955: Index for evaluating heat stress in terms of the resulting physiological strain. *Heat. Pip. Air Condit.* 27, 129–136.

Bell, F.W., 1978: *Food from the Sea: The Economics and Politics of Ocean Fisheries*. Westview Press, Boulder, Colo.

Beltzner, K. (ed.), 1976: *Living with Climatic Change*. Science Council of Canada, Ottawa.

Bentley, C.R., 1980: Response of the West Antarctic ice sheet to $CO_2$-induced climatic warming. Report of DOE sponsored meeting at Orono, Maine, June. (To be published as part of a AAAS study report).

Biggs, R.H. and J.F. Bartholic, 1973: Agronomic effects of climate change. In *Proceedings of the Second Conference on CIAP*, A.J. Broderick (ed.), U.S. Department of Transportation, Washington, D.C.

Bolin, B., 1979: Global ecology and man. In *Proceedings of the World Climate Conference*, WMO No. 537, World Meteorological Organization, Geneva, 27–50.

Bollman, F. and G. Hellyer, 1974: *The Economic Consequences of Projected Temperature Changes in Climatically Sensitive Wheat Growing Areas of the Canadian Prairie.* Development and Resources Corporation, Sacramento, Calif.

Brown, A.W., 1977: Yellow fever, dengue and dengue hemorrhagic fever. *A World Geography of Diseases,* G.M. Howe (ed.), Academic Press, London, 271–317.

Brown, L.R., with E.P. Eckholm, 1974: *By Bread Alone.* Praeger, New York.

Bryson, R.A. and T.J. Murray, 1977: *Climates of Hunger.* University of Wisconsin Press, Madison, Wisc.

Campbell, D.J., 1977: Strategies for coping with drought in the Sahel: A study of recent population movements in the department of Maradi, Niger. Ph.D. dissertation, Clark University, Worcester, Mass.

Carpenter, R., 1966: *Discontinuity in Greek Civilization.* Cambridge University Press, Cambridge.

Carr, H.P., 1949: Hookworm disease. In *Tice's Practice of Medicine* 5, W.F. Prior, Hagerstown, Md.

CEQ, 1979: *Environmental Quality.* The Tenth Annual Report of the Council on Environmental Quality, U.S. Gov't. Printing Office 041–011–00047–5, Washington, D.C.

CCTA/WHO, 1963: *African Conference on Ancyclostomiasis,* World Health Organization, Tech. Rept. Ser. No. 255, Geneva.

CIAP, 1975: Impacts of climatic change on the biosphere. Monograph 5, Part 2, September. Climatic Impact Assessment Program, U.S. Department of Transportation, Washington, D.C.

Clark, W.G., 1977: *The Lessons of the Peruvian Anchoveta Fishery.* California Cooperative Oceanic Fisheries Investigations, Reports XIX, 57–63.

Clawson, M., 1966: The influence of weather on outdoor recreation. In *Human Dimensions of Weather Modification,* W.R.D. Sewall (ed.), Dept. of Geography, Res. Paper No. 105, University of Chicago, 183–193.

Climate and Society Research Group, 1979: *The Effect of Climate Fluctuations on Human Populations:* Progress Report No. 2. Center for Technology, Environment, and Development, Clark University, Worcester, Mass.

Coakley, S.M., 1979: Climate variability in the Pacific Northwest and its effect on stripe rust disease of winter wheat. *Climatic Change 2*, 33–51.

Coan, E.V., J.N. Hillis and M. McCloskey, 1974: Strategies for international environmental action: The case for an environmentally oriented foreign policy. *Natural Resources J.* 14, 87–102.

Consolazio, C.F., R.E. Johnson and L.J. Pecora, 1963: *Physiological Measurements of Metabolic Functions in Man.* McGraw Hill, New York.

Cram, D., 1980: Hidden elements in the development and implementation of marine resource conservation policy: The case of the South West Africa/Namibian fisheries. In *Resource Management and Environmental Uncertainty: Lessons from Coastal Upwelling Fisheries,* M.H. Glantz and J.D. Thompson (eds.), John Wiley, New York.

Cramer, H.H., 1967: *Plant Protection and World Crop Production.* Leverkusen, West Germany.

Cushing, D.H., 1975: Marine Ecology and Fisheries. Cambridge University Press, Cambridge.

Cushing, D.H., 1979: Climatic variation and marine fisheries. In *Proceedings of the World Climate Conference,* WMO No. 537, World Meteorological Organization, Geneva, 608–637.

d'Arge, et al., 1975: *Economic and Social Measures of Biologic and Climatic Change.* Climatic Impact Assessment Program (CIAP) Monograph No. 6, U.S. Department of Transportation, Washington, D.C.

d'Arge, R.C., L. Eubanks and J. Barrington, 1976: *Benefit–Cost Analysis for Regulating Emissions of Fluorocarbons 11 and 12.* Final Report to U.S. Environmental Protection Agency, Contract 68–01–1918, University of Wyoming, Laramie.

d'Arge, R.C., 1979: Climate and economic activity. In *Proceedings of the World Climte Conference,* WMO No. 537, World Meteorological Organization, Geneva, 652–681.

94

d'Arge, R.C., W. Schulze, and D. Brookshire, 1980: *Benefit–cost valuation of long term future effects: The case of $CO_2$.* RFF/Climate Program Office Workshop on Methodology of Economic Impact Analysis for Climate Change, Ft. Lauderdale, Fla. (in press).

Dasman, R.F., 1972: *Environmental Conservation.* John Wiley, New York.

DeLancey, M.W., 1978: Health and disease on the plantations of Cameroon. In *Disease in African History*, G.W. Hartwig and K.D. Patterson (eds.), Duke University Press, Durham, N.C.

DOE, 1979: *Workshop on Environmental and Societal Consequences of a Possible $CO_2$-Induced Climate Change.* Annapolis, Md., 2–6 April, U.S. Dept. of Energy, Washington, D.C.

Falk, R.A., 1971: *The Endangered Planet: Prospects and Proposals for Human Survival.* Random House, New York.

Falkenmark, M. and G. Lindh, 1976: *Water for a Starving World.* Westview Press, Boulder, Colo.

FAO, 1978: *Fishery Products: Supply, Demand and Trade Projections to 1985.* ESC:PROJ/79/5, June, Food and Agriculture Organizations, Rome.

FAO, 1979: FAO Production Yearbook. Statistics Series No. 22, Vol. 32, Food and Agriculture Organization, Rome.

Flohn, H., 1950: Klimaschwankungen im Mittelalter und ihre historisch–geographische Bedeutung. *Berichte zur dt. Landeskunde 7*, 347–357.

Flohn, H., and S. Nicholson, 1980: Climatic fluctuations in the arid belt of the "old world" since the last glacial maximum: Possible causes and future implications. In *Paleoecology of Africa and the Surrounding Islands*, Vol. 12, M. Sarnthein, E. Seibold, and R. Rognon (eds.), A.A. Balkema Publ., Rotterdam, Netherlands, 3–21.

Gerasimov, I. P., 1979: Climates of past geological epochs. In *Proceedings of the World Climate Conference*, WMO No. 537, World Meteorological Organization, Geneva, 88–111.

Glantz, M.H., 1979: Science, politics and economics of the Peruvian anchoveta fishery. *Marine Policy*, July, 201–210.

Green, J.S., 1967: Holiday meteorology: Reflections on weather and outdoor comfort. *Weather* 27, 128–131.

Griffitt, W., 1970: Environmental effects on interpersonal affective behavior: Ambient effective temperature and attraction. *Representative Research in Social Psychology* 1, 33–48.

Harrison, P., 1979: The curse of the tropics. *New Scientist* 84, 602–604.

Heady, E.O., et al, 1973: National and interregional models of water demand, land use, and agricultural policies. *Water Resources Research*, 9, 777–791.

Hendrick, R., 1965: *Potential Impact of Weather Modification on the Insurance Industry*. Travelers Research Center, Hartford, Conn.

Hentschel, G., 1964: Sports and climate. In *Medical Climatology*, S. Light and H.L. Kameretz (eds.), Waverly Press, Baltimore, Md.

Hjul, P., 1977: World fish stocks on a delicate balance. *Geographic Mag.* October, 27–37.

Houghton, R.G., 1980: Fish and chips: Rise and fall of England's cod fishing. *Oceans* March, 58–61.

House of Representatives, 1978: *Weather Impacts on the Budget and Economy*, Task Force on Community and Physical Resources of the Committee on the Budget, House of Representatives, U.S. Gov't. Printing Office TF–7–95–36, Washington, D.C.

Howe, C.W., 1980: *An overview of conceptual and methodological issues arising in climate impact assessment and policy formulation*. RFF/Climate Program Office Workshop on Methodology of Economic Impact Analysis for Climate Change, Ft. Lauderdale, Fla. (in press).

Kamarck, A.M., 1976: *The Tropics and Economic Development*. Johns Hopkins University Press, Baltimore, Md.

Kellogg, W.W., 1978: Global influences of mankind on the climate. In *Climatic Change*, J. Gribbin (ed.), Cambridge University Press, Cambridge, 205–227.

Kernan, G.F., 1970: To prevent a world wasteland: A proposal. *Foreign Affairs* 48, 401–413.

Koch, L., 1945: The East Greenland ice. *Medd. om Grønland* 130, Copenhagen.

Lamb, H.H., 1977: *Climates: Present, Past and Future.* 2 vols., Methuen, London.

Learmonth, A., 1977: Malaria. In *A World Geography of Human Disease,* G.M. Howe (ed.), Academic Press, London.

Lieth, H., 1973: Primary production: Terrestrial ecosystems, *Human Ecology* 1, 303–332.

Lovins, A.G., 1980: Economically efficient energy futures. In *Interactions of Energy and Climate,* W. Bach, J. Pankrath, and J. Williams (eds.), Reidel, Dordrecht, Netherlands, 1–32; see also Lovins, A.G., 1977: *Soft Energy Paths: Toward a Durable Peace,* Friends of the Earth Intl., Ballinger, Cambridge, Mass.

May, J.M., 1958: *The Ecology of Human Disease.* MD Publications, New York.

McFadden, D., 1980: *Welfare analysis of incomplete adjustment to climate change.* RFF/Climate Program Office Workshop on Methodology of Economic Impact Analysis for Climate Change, Ft. Lauderdale, Fla. (in press).

McKay, G.A., and T. Allsopp, 1980: The role of climate in affecting energy demand/supply. In *Interactions of Energy and Climate,* W. Bach, J. Pankrath, and J. Williams (eds.), Reidel, Dordrecht, Netherlands, 53–72.

McKerslake, D., 1972: *The Stress of Hot Environments.* Cambridge University Press, Cambridge.

Mooney, P.R., 1979: *Seeds of the Earth: A Private or Public Resource?* International Coalition for Development Action, London.

More, R.J., 1967: Hydrological models and geography. In *Models in Geography,* R.J. Chorley and P. Haggett (eds.), Methuen, London.

Mortara, G., 1967: Factors affecting rural–urban migration in Latin America: Influence of economic and social conditions in these two areas. In *Proceedings of the World Population Conference,* IV, United Nations, New York, 509–512.

Mosaic, 1975: All that unplowed sea. Vol. 6, May–June, 22–27.

Myers, N., 1979: *The Sinking Ark: A New Look at the Problem of Disappearing Species.* Pergamon Press, New York.

NAS, 1962: *Tropical Health: A Report on a Study of Needs and Resources.* National Academy of Sciences, Washington, D.C.

NAS, 1972: *Genetic Vulnerability of Major Crops.* National Academy of Sciences, Washington, D.C.

NAS, 1976: *Climate and Food: Climatic Fluctuation and U.S. Agricultural Production.* Committee on Climate and Weather Fluctuations and Agricultural Production, National Academy of Sciences, Washington, D.C.

NAS, 1977a: *Energy and Climate.* Studies in Geophysics, National Academy of Sciences, Washington, D.C.

NAS, 1977b: *Food and Nutrition Study.* National Academy of Sciences, Washington, D.C.

National Climatic Center, 1979: *State, Regional, and National Monthly and Annual Temperatures Weighted by Area.* NOAA, Asheville, N.C.

Nelson, G., 1970: We need a new global agency to confront the environment crisis. In *War and Peace Report* 10, 3–5.

Nichols, H., 1975: *Palynological and Paleoclimatic Study of the Late Quaternary Displacement of the Boreal Forest–Tundra Ecotone in Keewatin and Mackenzie, N.W.T., Canada,* Occasional Paper No. 15, Inst. of Arctic and Alpine Res., University of Colorado, Boulder, Colo.

Oguntoyinbo, S. and R.S. Odingo, 1979: Climatic variability and land use: An African perspective. In *Proceedings of the World Climate Conference,* WMO No. 537, Geneva, 552–580.

Oliver, J.E., 1973: *Climate and Man's Environment.* John Wiley, New York.

Parry, M.L., 1978: *Climatic Change, Agriculture and Settlement.* Dawson, Folkestone, England.

Parsons, H.M., 1979: Temperature and motivation. *Trans. Amer. Soc. Heating, Refrigeration and Air–Conditioning Engineers* 85, Part I, 768–774.

Patterson, D.K. and G.W. Hartwig, 1978: The disease factor: An introductory overview. In *Disease in African History,* G.W. Hartwig and K.D. Patterson (eds.), Duke University Press, Durham, N.C.

Paul, A.H., 1972: Weather and the daily use of outdoor recreation in Canada. In *Weather Forecasting for Agriculture and Industry, A Symposium,* J.A. Taylor and N. Abbot (eds.), David and Charles, Devon, England.

Perry, A.H., 1972: Weather, climate, and tourism. *Weather* 27, 199–203.

Pimentel, D. and M. Pimentel, 1978: Dimensions of the world food problem and losses to pests. In *World Food, Pest Losses, and the Environment.* D. Pimentel (ed.), Westview Press, Boulder, Colo., 1–16.

Quirk, W.D. and J.E. Moriarty, 1980: Prospects for using improved climate information to better manage energy systems. In *Interactions of Energy and Climate,* W. Bach, J. Pankrath, and J. Williams (eds.), Reidel, Dordrecht, Netherlands, 89–99.

Radovich, J. 1980: The collapse of the California sardine fishery: What have we learned? In *Resource Management and Environmental Uncertainty: Lessons from Coastal Upwelling Fisheries,* M.H. Glantz and J.D. Thompson (eds.) John Wiley, New York.

Ramirez, J.M., C.M. Sakamoto and R.E. Jensen, 1975: Wheat. In *Impacts of Climatic Change on the Biosphere,* CIAP Monograph 5, Part 2, September. Climatic Impact Assessment Program, U.S. Dept. of Transportation, Washington, D.C.

Rée, G., 1977: Schistosomiasis. In *A World Geography of Human Diseases,* G.M. Howe (ed.), Academic Press, London.

Roberts, W.O., 1980: Contending with climate. In *Food and Climate Review 1979,* Aspen Institute for Humanistic Studies, Boulder, Colo., 3–13.

Rogers, L., 1928: The incidence and spread of cholera in India: Forecasting and control epidemics. *Indian Med. Res.* 9.

Rohles, F.H., 1970: The model comfort envelope: A new approach toward defining the thermal environment in which sedentary man is comfortable. Paper presented at the ASHRAE Annual Meeting, Kansas City, Mo., 28 June–1 July, No. 2165.

Russell, A.J. and J. Sundaranajan, 1928: The epidemiology of cholera in India. *Indian Med. Res.* 12.

Ryther, J.H., 1969: Photosynthesis and fish production in the sea. *Science,* 166, 72–76.

Schneider, S.H. and R.S. Chen, 1980: Carbon dioxide warming and coastline flooding: Physical factors and climatic impact. *Ann. Rev. Energy* 5, 107–140.

Schwartz, H.E., 1977: Climatic change and water supply: How sensitive is the Northeast? In *Climate, Climatic Change, and Water Supply*, National Academy of Sciences, Washington, D.C.

Smith, E.K., 1980: *Economic Impact Analysis and Climate Change: An overview and proposed research agenda.* RFF/Climate Program Office Workshop on Methodology of Economic Impact Analysis for Climate Change, Ft. Lauderdale, Fla. (in press).

Sorenson, B., 1975: Energy and resources, *Science*, 180, 225–260.

Stidd, C.K., 1976: Tradewinds and soybeans. *Oceans* July, 30–33.

Stigler, G.J., 1939: Production and distribution in the short run. *J. Political Econ.* 47, 305–327.

Swaminathan, M.S., 1979: Global aspects of food production. In *Proceedings of the World Climate Conference*, WMO No. 537, World Meteorological Organization, Geneva, 369–405.

Tannehill, I.R., 1947: *Drought, its Causes and Effects.* Princeton University Press, Princeton.

Thompson, L.M., 1975: Weather variability, climatic change and grain production. *Science* 188, 535–541.

TIE, 1980: *The Role of Organic Soils in the World Carbon Cycle.* Rept. of Workshop in Indianapolis, Ind., May 1979, sponsored by DOE, The Inst. of Ecology, Indianapolis, Ind. (DOE, CONF–7905135, UC–11).

UNFPA, 1979: *World Population Policies.* United Nations Fund for Population Activities, J.S. Singh (ed.), Praeger, New York.

USDA, 1964: Soil Conservation Service, Northern Plains States, Estimated Total Annual Yield: Being the 2nd approximation of average natural productivity of range sites. Lincoln, Nebr.

VanDyne, G.M. and D.F. Pendleton, 1980: *Research Issues in Grazinglands under Changing Climate.* Rept. prepared for DOE sponsored Climate Project of the American Association for the Advancement of Science, Washington, D.C.

Vernon, H.M., 1932: The measurement of radiant heat in relation to human comfort. *J. Industrial Hygiene* 14, 95–111.

Vernon, R., 1968: Economic sovereignty at bay. *Foreign Affairs* 47, 110–122.

Vondruska, J., 1980: Postwar production, consumption, and price of fish meal. In *Resource Management and Environmental Uncertainty: Lessons from Coastal Upwelling Fisheries*, M.H. Glantz and J.D. Thompson (eds.), John Wiley, New York.

Weihe, W., 1979: Climate, health, and disease. In *Proceedings of the World Climate Conference*, WMO No. 537, World Meteorological Organization, Geneva, 313–368.

Whittaker, R.H., 1975: *Communities and Ecosystems.* Macmillan, New York.

WHO, 1971: *WHO Expert Committee on Yellow Fever.* WHO Tech. Rept. No. 479, World Health Organization, Geneva.

WHO, 1977: *Infectious Diseases: Cases and Deaths.* World Health Organization, Geneva.

Wijmstra, T.A., 1979: Paleobotany and climate change. In *Climatic Change*, J. Gribbin (ed.), Cambridge University Press, Cambridge, 25–45.

Wittfogel, K.A., 1957: *Oriental Despotism.* Yale University Press, New Haven, Conn.

Wittwer, S.H., 1980: Carbon dioxide and climatic change: An agricultural perspective. *J. Soil and Water Conservation* 35, 116–120.

WMO, 1980: *Outline and Basis for the World Climate Programme 1980–1983*, WMO No. 540, World Meteorological Organization, Geneva.

# IV. POLICY DECISIONS AND MEASURES DEALING WITH THE CARBON DIOXIDE/CLIMATE PROBLEM

## 1. Long Range Strategies

Societies are faced with the problem of coping with both short term climatic fluctuations or extreme events, and the longer term gradual climatic change induced by carbon dioxide. In order to reduce the effects of adverse climatic impacts from both causes, simultaneous planning and design will have to take place in a number of different sectors including agriculture, water and energy resources, land use, and fisheries. Action is needed now to diminish the adverse impacts of natural climatic fluctuations, particularly in regions and countries highly susceptible to these fluctuations. In doing so we may also decrease vulnerability to climatic changes induced by mankind.

While there are many long range strategies that may lead to increased resiliency (some of which are discussed in Chapter III), there are also certain obstacles to responding effectively to impending climatic changes. Among the more obvious are the following:

### 1.1 Incomplete information

What policy makers would like, beyond the very general statement that mankind is likely to face markedly different distributions of climate in 20 years, are detailed predictions of the magnitude and timing of the changes and how they will affect economic and political processes. Barring a major breakthrough, however, such information seems far off (see Sections II.4 and III.1).

Meteorologists use complex computer models of the climate system, supplemented by studies of past climates, to understand how increasing carbon dioxide may affect the atmosphere, oceans, and land. But even though there is some general agreement about the range of estimates of global average temperature rise for a doubling of carbon dioxide ($3°\pm1.5°C$), important and nagging uncertainties remain, as discussed in Chapter II. Perhaps the greatest deficiency in our information about the future climate is our inability to predict temperatures and precipitation on a *regional* scale. We are also uncertain about when such changes would occur.

Furthermore, there is the prospect of a sea level rise due to disintegration of one or more ice sheets. But, again, there is disagreement about the time scale of such an event.

Thus, the public and policy makers who must interpret public opinion are faced with a set of seemingly remote problems about which information is still incomplete. It is not surprising that they tend to delay, until more details of the future are known, major commitments to long range strategies that would mitigate the effects of climate change.

## 1.2   Poor planning and information distribution

Political and industrial leaders are often forced to plan for the future in the face of uncertainties. Good planning requires that they have adequate information on which to base decisions; for the carbon dioxide problem policy makers must know what sort of climate to expect, in both the near and distant future. This is the purpose of the World Climate Data and Applications Programmes, recently instituted as components of the World Climate Programme.

The collapse of the British peanut crop in Tanzania in 1949 illustrates how useful climatological data could have been in making long term plans for this weather sensitive enterprise. Climate information shows that the area was irresponsibly selected; it requires extensive irrigation to even remain viable (Yao, 1973; Sakamoto et al., 1979). Adequate planning using this climatic information could have averted the losses.

A case of a government failing to supply adequate environmental information is that of Sri Lanka (Hewapathirane, 1977). There, over 60 percent of the urban residents who resettled in a rural area were not told that they had moved into a flood zone. In another case, tropical storm Agnes galvanized some U.S. citizens to take legal action against the federal government for not adequately disseminating information concerning the availability of government flood insurance (Burton et al., 1978).

More generally, it has been argued that many of the developing nations have become increasingly vulnerable to climate changes for the following reason: Colonialism disrupted indigenous cultures and haphazardly imposed investment choices, construction, and water resource developments, which turned out to enhance sensitivity to climatic fluctuations (Baird, 1975; Oguntoyinbo and Odingo, 1979).

## 1.3 Discounting the future

People often discount their future more heavily than serves their own long range advantage. Many people prefer to bear the "evils" they know rather than plan ahead to protect against those they do not yet know. Near rewards, if even unsure and only temporary, are generally preferable to more distant benefits (Kellogg and Mead, 1977). Psychological studies show that the perception of risk by individuals — as well as whole societies — is very distorted. For example, despite contrary evidence, flood victims have denied the risks of floods ever recurring in their area (Kates, 1962). Even residents in relatively high risk hazard areas, such as flood and earthquake zones, have been extremely reluctant to purchase insurance protection, even when the protection is heavily subsidized by the government.

If we are to satisfy the concerns about future carbon dioxide-induced climatic changes, governments should begin incorporating and making better use of the available climatological knowledge in planning and designing climate sensitive activities. Policy makers should see that information about climatic change, as it affects human activities, is applied appropriately (see Section III.1).

We may hypothesize that if the following conditions are at least partially met, most societies would probably become increasingly resilient to climatic impacts from a carbon dioxide-induced warming, regardless of their natural environments, levels of economic production, and cultural development. Accordingly, a society should:

- Recognize the problem of increased carbon dioxide production and climate change, and take it seriously enough to be considered in the political process;
- Plan for both short term (e.g., disaster relief) and long term (e.g., economic conversion) changes;
- Make use of state-of-the-art climate data for planning in agriculture, land use, and energy and water resource development, to name a few;
- Plan and implement warning systems and disseminate forecasts;
- Maintain food reserves;
- Diversify agricultural and energy practices.

While these suggestions may seem to be common sense, history shows that some societies have failed to recognize this and have responded differently to similar climatic perturbations. For example, both Ireland and the Netherlands experienced long, wet winters and potato blights in the 1840s. This had a dramatic impact on the Irish and triggered widespread famine, death, and emigration. But the Dutch were able to minimize the impacts of the disaster, due in part to a more flexible and diversified economy (Rabb, 1980; Mokyr, 1980).

Patterns of economic development (including distribution of resources among the population, occupational structure, and the world food and commodity markets) have mediated the effects of climatic perturbations in another case. The droughts that occurred in the Sahel around 1973 and Great Britain in 1976 had quite disparate effects. In the Sahelian drought thousands of children died of malnutrition; a few deaths in Great Britain would have been considered a national scandal (Garcia, 1980). By contrasting these and other climatic events we may find the specific characteristics of different socioeconomic systems that make them more resilient or more vulnerable to climatic perturbations.

## 2. Averting the Change

Measures to avert carbon dioxide–induced climatic changes fall into three categories: reduce demand for fossil fuels, especially by conserving and using alternative energy resources; adopt technical solutions to collect and sequester carbon dioxide emissions; and increase biomass, including reforesting denuded areas. To be of significant value, however, such measures must be taken worldwide, since the problem is a global one; action by one or two countries alone would have little influence on the buildup of carbon dioxide.

### 2.1 Reduce fossil fuel demand

According to the recent report of the National Research Council's Committee on Nuclear and Alternative Energy Systems (NRC, 1979b): "Conservation deserves the highest immediate priority in energy planning."

This is a conclusion that has been reiterated in several studies of the economic and environmental risks involved in the United States' energy future (Marshall, 1980). Comparisons with other countries, for instance, show that the per capita use of energy (about 10 kilowatts) is much greater in the U.S. than in most other countries that have similar per capita incomes but different national "energy efficiency" policies (Darmstadter et al., 1977; Schipper and Lichtenberg, 1976). These variations can readily be seen in Figure IV.1.

A recent Harvard University study (Stobaugh and Yergin, 1979), concluded that conservation measures in the United States could result in 30 to 40 percent reductions in energy consumption with

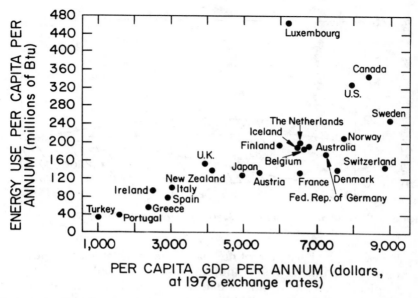

**Figure IV.1.** Correlation between per capita energy use and gross domestic product per annum for various industrialized countries (OECD, 1978).

"virtually no penalty for the way Americans live." Already improvements in energy efficiency in the U.S. have resulted in a 10 percent reduction in the energy used per unit of GNP; this may fall by 30 percent by the end of the century (Marshall, 1980).

In addition to conservation, Amory Lovins (1977) recommends we follow "soft energy paths" that can minimize carbon dioxide emissions in the future. These soft paths combine conservation measures with use of renewable energy sources such as solar, wind, and geothermal power that are locally controlled. Lovins illustrates (Figure IV.2.) how soft energy paths might meet virtually all of the United States' energy needs in the next 50 years. In addition, conservation measures would make more cheaper energy available in the future, increase goods and services delivered per unit of energy used, and minimize fossil fuel combustion (Daly, 1979; NRC, 1979a; Schipper, 1976; Hitch, 1978).

So-called "hard energy paths," such as fission and fusion, could serve as long term energy sources. The choice of nuclear technologies has a clear advantage over fossil fuels as far as carbon dioxide emissions are concerned (see Appendix A).

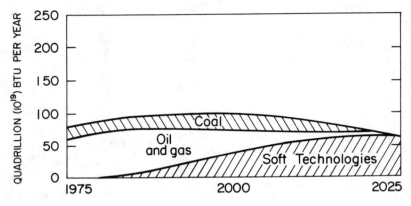

**Figure IV.2. An alternate future for U.S. gross energy use (Lovins, 1977).**

However, the hard path of nuclear power may, at least in the short term, be an unacceptable one; increasingly the public is becoming suspicious of the health and environmental risks involved and uncertain about the availability of uranium. But it is not the purpose of this report to analyze the concern and controversy surrounding long range hazards of nuclear power as an energy resource. Technical assessments of such costs and risks have been made elsewhere (NRC, 1979a; 1979b; NAS, 1979; Holdren, 1977; Sagan, 1972; Pochin, 1976).

The essential point here is that reducing energy demand, as many have advocated, will reduce both the burning of fossil fuels and a reliance on nuclear energy. These are two good reasons for justifying energy conservation as a cornerstone of the energy policies of the U.S. and other developed countries. To significantly affect the global production of carbon dioxide, however, such measures would have to be adopted by all major users of fossil fuels. We will return to this point in Sections 4 and 5.

## 2.2 Technical solutions

Several technical solutions have been proposed for managing the carbon dioxide produced by burning fossil fuels. These solutions seek to control the atmospheric concentration of carbon dioxide, thereby averting its possible climatic impacts.

Ultimately the success of these methods is linked with world energy policies, forest management, and personal and societal values. The costs involved must be considered; they are fundamental to any discussion of the technical carbon dioxide solutions proposed so far. Whether the world will have the surpluses in energy, capital, and manpower required to adopt any one of the possible solutions is unclear, even if such extreme measures were deemed desirable.

The most economical solution would be to control carbon dioxide emissions at their source. To do this effectively, efforts would have to be concentrated on the large fossil fuel producing or consuming facilities. Marchetti (1977) points out that 80 percent of coal and virtually all oil pass through centralized processing facilities such as refineries and power plants before being burned. He argues that we have easy access to the carbon dioxide produced in the plants and should take steps to control it there.

However, three problems emerge in connection with the proposal. First, although we could recover carbon dioxide produced in refining processes, the bulk of it is released at the point of combustion, typically in transportation applications. Therefore it is extremely difficult to control. Second, there are considerable technical and financial problems associated with controlling emissions from power plants (some of which are discussed in more detail below). Third, if we wish to completely control and manage carbon dioxide emissions, the only effective procedure would probably require centralizing complex, large scale production facilities and converting societies to an all-electric or hydrogen economy. This could indeed make all carbon dioxide accessible to recovery methods but would, in turn, involve substantial social changes, not to mention extravagant costs associated with developing the necessary infrastructures. Willingness to undertake this sort of technical solution would depend on the predicted costs relative to the perceived benefits of avoiding a change in climate. Marchetti (1977) estimates that 50 percent of the carbon dioxide produced in any large facility could be recovered, although high estimates (up to 99 percent) have been calculated in other studies.

Assuming we could control carbon dioxide emissions, the next step would be to dispose of it. The first step in this process is to determine whether all stack gases or just carbon dioxide should be discarded. Energy invested to isolate and collect carbon dioxide from the other gases would likely prove beneficial, since a relatively small volume would then have to be disposed. This is accomplished with a straightforward method of capturing carbon dioxide through the use of absorbent materials. They selectively capture the carbon dioxide which is then released when the absorber is heated. Many such absorbers have been considered, according to Mustacchi et al. (1978), and Hoffert et al. (1979).

Once it is readied for disposal, long term storage of carbon dioxide can be a problem. The most commonly discussed storage location is the deep ocean. The carbon dioxide could be injected at several points in the oceans where natural currents would encourage transport and diffusion into bottom waters and sediments. Given the right temperature and pressure, carbon dioxide becomes a liquid more dense than water. Introduced into the ocean as a liquid it would sink to the deepest point and remain there (Marchetti, 1977). Even a sea water and carbon dioxide mixture might be more dense than water. It would have the added advantage of not requiring injection as deep as a pure carbon dioxide liquid (Baes et al., 1980). Dry ice dropped from the sea surface in suitable packages has also been suggested as a method for carbon dioxide disposal.

There are several areas that might be suitable for introducing carbon dioxide into the ocean. The Straits of Gibralter is one site, as first suggested by Marchetti (1977). Flow rates from the Mediterranean Sea seem adequate to carry a large amount of carbon out into the deep Atlantic Ocean. The current that flows from the Mediterranean is more dense than Atlantic waters, so it sinks to depths that guarantee a long residence time for any carbon dioxide carried with it. The carbon involved is thus removed for periods of at least several centuries. Clearly, more than one such ocean site needs to be identified if the global production of carbon dioxide is to be disposed of in this way. Other possible locations include the Red Sea and the polar Weddell and Norwegian Seas.

There are shortcomings to the ocean disposal solution. First, storage in the oceans can affect the rate of increase of carbon dioxide but not the ultimate value of the atmospheric concentration, since oceanic and atmospheric carbon levels will eventually come to equilibrium. If all carbon resources are eventually burned, the atmospheric concentration will, far in the future, exceed 1000 parts per million by volume (ppmv) — which is more than three times the preindustrial value (Hoffert et al., 1979). Second, the proposed oceanic disposal methods require that ocean currents be constant and predictable in order to carry carbon dioxide to deep waters. Gibrat (1978) indicates that the currents in the regions cited above are subject to the influence of tides and atmospheric wind and pressure variations. They also have characteristic turbulence patterns whose changes with time are impossible to predict.

Alternatives to carbon dioxide extraction from stack gases include pumping all the flue gases including carbon dioxide into the ocean, and trapping the carbon dioxide in sea water and then pumping the sea water to the bottom of the ocean. Mustacchi et al. (1978) estimate that electricity costs would be doubled for disposal of all flue gases. This estimate is challenged, however, by Steinberg and Albanese (1980). They suggest that a 60 to 90 percent recovery through the sea water capture method would require so much energy that more carbon dioxide would be produced in the process than could be captured. Scrubbers currently in use for carbon dioxide are highly energy consumptive; unless they are made more efficient, all the power plant output would be required to recover the carbon dioxide (Dyson and Marland, 1979).

Transporting gases over land to disposal sites is also expensive. In order to cut these costs power plants would have to be situated along the few shorelines that are close to suitable deep ocean storage regions. Baes et al. (1980) suggest using floating power plants; these could be cooled by sea water and could be conveniently located for carbon dioxide disposal.

Another approach to carbon dioxide disposal might be to put it back where it came from — geological formations from which oil and gas have been removed (Marchetti, 1977; 1979). However, the long term stability of these areas is questionable because of the different chemical characteristics of carbon dioxide and the natural gas or oil it would replace.

One other method of sequestering carbon dioxide is discussed by Dyson and Marland (1979) in which separation of carbon dioxide from either the atmosphere or from stack gases could be followed by processing it with heat and water to produce carbon fuels. The heat would come from nuclear or solar power stations. The resulting carbon fuels could be substituted for fossil resources, thereby removing carbon dioxide from the atmosphere and reducing eventual emissions. An immense number of nuclear or solar energy stations would be required to absorb the current rate of global carbon dioxide emissions. This scheme would require 5700 1000–megawatt plants, which would not only tax the financial resources of the globe but would probably require using the world's supply of important metals. This plan also presents a major waste heat problem that could change the climate.

## 2.3  Increase biomass, including reforestation

Instead of disposing of carbon dioxide there are ways to expand the natural sinks that absorb it. For instance, Cooper (1978) points out that an increase of just 1 percent in the plant life on Earth, especially the forests, would be sufficient to absorb one year's release of carbon dioxide at the present rate. However, if the carbon dioxide release continues to increase at about 4 percent per year, the increase in biomass required to absorb the extra load would be 2 percent after 17 years — probably an unreasonable level. In short, the more fossil fuel we use the less effective the biomass sink becomes.

Only if two criteria are met can expanding the world's biomass help control atmospheric carbon dioxide levels. First, sufficient resources (such as land, water, nutrients, manpower, and capital) must be available to encourage the growth of vegetation whose net yearly carbon uptake would keep pace with the yearly increase in emissions. Second, disposal methods must be found that will sequester fixed (organic) carbon for long periods.

Several possibilities exist. One is to spread nitrogen and phosphorus on the surface of the ocean to encourage algae growth. After passing through the food chain, these plants would deposit carbon on the ocean bottom (Dyson and Marland, 1979). The ecological consequences of this scheme are unknown, and a significant expansion of the oceanic sink in this manner seems unlikely.

The nitrogen and phosphorus fertilizers used to grow algae could be used to grow trees instead, thereby fixing carbon. More than half of the mass of the living biosphere is contained in the tropical forests (Loomis, 1979). But a great number of trees would be involved, perhaps covering 1 percent of the area of present forests each year, which could pose other significant environmental problems. For instance, at least part of the land suitable for such planting is already in use. And much potentially serviceable land is already being exploited by those who want to deforest it for agriculture and grazing. But assuming we want to rely on the biomass as a carbon dioxide sink, we would need to identify areas that are of sufficient size and could be successfully planted.

The problem of disposing of all this organic carbon would still remain, however. Short of creating ever increasing forests, the plant material could be processed to create carbon rich gases such as methane for storage in geological reservoirs or used as substitutes for fossil fuel. However, converting biomass to methanol or liquid fuels requires an energy investment. Considering the scale of the above reforestation effort, the use of energy to convert biomass to fuel would probably involve enormous resources and might exacerbate the carbon dioxide problem. Additionally, the energy transportation infrastructure would have to be considerably expanded, since the carbon presently carried out of mines and wells as oil, gas, and coal would reappear in complex and heavier forms of biomass such as wood (Dyson and Marland, 1979).

The ecological implications of the reforestation schemes cannot be overlooked. In fact additional climatic consequences may result, since changed vegetation patterns could offset the intended cooling effect by absorbing more solar radiation, thus warming the Earth (Marchetti, 1979).

## 3. Mitigating the Effects

The uncertainties inherent in the carbon dioxide problem are often cited as justification for taking no action now. But whether carbon dioxide builds up or not, we know that weather and climate will continue to fluctuate greatly. Dealing with the carbon dioxide/climate problem is one way of coping with climatic variability in general. Thus, we have strong incentives to: reduce the vulnerability of human settlements and activities to both climatic variability and change; begin actions to mitigate adverse carbon dioxide–induced impacts; and take advantage of the beneficial effects.

Most of the measures that will protect us from gradual carbon dioxide–induced changes will probably benefit us in the short term as well because natural climatic variations are always occurring. This conclusion has been reinforced by case studies in both developing and developed countries and in recent international meetings on carbon dioxide and global climatic change. In this section we highlight a few strategies that will help to increase our resilience and mitigate the effects of global climate change; they will likely be advantageous even if no climate change occurs. Moreover, some of these strategies may also slow the increase in atmospheric carbon dioxide.

Table IV.1 lists the specific mitigating strategies that will be discussed. These seem to be the most important ones to pursue immediately; some of them have already been adopted in a limited way.

### 3.1 Strategies that increase resilience to climatic change

● *Protect arable soil.*   The loss of arable soil through erosion or salinization has been partly responsible for the decline of entire civilizations in the past (Carter and Dale, 1974). Currently as much land globally is being lost to agriculture

**Table IV.1.**   Strategies to mitigate the effects of increased atmospheric carbon dioxide, or to help to avert the climate change.

| Strategies that: | | |
|---|---|---|
| **Increase resilience** | **Reduce $CO_2$ emissions** | **Improve choices** |
| Protect arable soil | Energy conservation | Environmental monitoring and warning |
| Improve water management | Renewable energy resources | Provision of improved climate data and its application |
| Apply agrotechnology | Reforestation | |
| Coastal land use policies | | Public information and education |
| Maintain global food reserves | | Transfer appropriate technology |
| Disaster relief | | |

due to poor management practices as is being opened up (Kovda, 1980). To maintain or increase worldwide food production soil must be protected. This is especially important in marginal, semi–arid lands where overgrazing and poor agricultural practices have led to desertification (Glantz, 1977; Oguntoyinbo and Odingo, 1979). The process is accelerated during periods of drought.

- *Improve water management.* Building dams, aqueducts, reservoirs, irrigation systems, and diverting rivers are all techniques that can provide an adequate and reliable water supply in times of drought and can protect against river flooding. These techniques are well developed; they must be applied with an intimate knowledge of the statistics of rainfall and runoff — that is, the climate (Schaake and Kaczmarek, 1979).

- *Apply agrotechnology.* The supply and adequate distribution of food will continue to be a major problem for the world. Agrotechnology, which led to the "Green Revolution", has permitted more food to be grown in many areas. But the monocultures that account for most of our food (see Section III.3) are generally more susceptible to both short and

114

long term climate changes than are diversified crops. Thus, we will need to develop such agrotechnologies as more efficient irrigation systems, salt water crops, new forms of nitrogen fixing plants, and plants that will be adapted to changing climates expected in food growing regions (see Section II.4). It may take special crops such as sorghum, millet, maize, and sesame to thrive in semi–arid areas. These are generally well adapted to the average climate of the tropical regions where they are grown, but they can be sensitive to climate variability there (Mattei, 1979). Agrotechnology can also exploit useful plants such as the versatile tree *leucaena leucocephala*, dubbed "the schmoo tree" (Time, 1979).

● *Improve coastal land use policies.*   Floods, hurricanes, and typhoons cause environmental and property damage, and loss of human lives. This destruction has been extreme in coastal areas throughout the world (Kates, 1980). Much planning in coastal regions has been carried out without adequate application of climatic data. If coastal communities are to effectively mitigate adverse weather and climate events, this information must be used when proposing land use programs. A future sea level rise is one more factor that should be part of this planning even though its timing is still uncertain (see Section II.3).

● *Maintain global food reserves.*   The growing world population will require a reliable food supply. Since any future temperature or precipitation shifts could adversely affect major food producing regions, it would be prudent to be prepared with adequate food reserves (Schneider with Mesirow, 1976).

● *Provide disaster relief.*   International relief organizations can help countries better cope with short term climatic variations and long term climatic changes. However, in recent years relief efforts have been viewed suspiciously; some believe they have been conducted in pursuit of national interests (Garcia, 1980).

## 3.2   Strategies that reduce carbon dioxide emissions

● *Conserve energy.*   A low growth energy future would mean that carbon dioxide–induced environmental impacts could be largely avoided. There are strong incentives to conserve, including reducing dependence on OPEC oil, and protecting the environment (CEQ, 1979). Conservation is one part of the "soft energy path" (see Section IV.2) that can result in more energy efficiency. It requires a more extensive use of renewable energy resources. However, in order to achieve a significant reduction in carbon dioxide emissions this strategy would have to be adopted by most countries of the world.

● *Use renewable energy resources.*  These include: wood and other biomass substances; nuclear fission reactors that "breed" plutonium fuel; nuclear fusion reactors that use virtually limitless hydrogen found in water; garbage; wind; and solar energy, which includes direct capture of sunlight, hydroelectric power, and ocean thermal sources. There are tradeoffs related to each of these energy forms: some are less risky and less polluting than others, and some produce more net energy for a given capital investment.

● *Reforest.*  To some extent all countries depend on wood for fuel and construction material. More than half of the mass of the entire biosphere is in the tropical forests of the world. Some reports indicate that these forests are being reduced by as much as 1 percent per year (see Section II.2), although this information is not very reliable. Such widespread deforestation ruins a valuable economic asset. But in India, Nepal, Sri Lanka, Brazil, and parts of Africa, removal of the forest cover has also degraded the soil and caused severe erosion. However, many countries have instituted reforestation projects (CEQ, 1980), and this is a hopeful sign. As pointed out in Sections II.2 and IV.2, a regrowth of trees takes up atmospheric carbon dioxide and converts it to plant tissue through photosynthesis. Thus, reforestation is not only a strategy that makes sense in economic terms, it also provides a sink for the carbon dioxide we are releasing (see Section IV.2).

### 3.3  Strategies that lead to improved choices

● *Employ environmental monitoring and warning systems.*  As described in Section IV.4, acquisition of climate data and global monitoring of the environment are functions of the World Meteorological Organization (WMO) and the U.N. Environmental Programme. Thus, we are able to keep track of the environment of our planet, despite some gaps in the coverage, such as conditions below the ocean surface, the

116

size and shape of the ice sheets of Greenland and the Antarctic, and the state of the tropical forests.

- *Provide and apply improved climate data.*  Climate data have been gathered at many stations throughout the world, but only a small part of it is available in readily usable forms, notably in some developing countries. The data needs for applied climatology have been well defined by the WMO's Commission for Special Applications of Meteorology and Climatology. But expert help and financial assistance are needed to locate and process it into punch cards and magnetic tapes for computer use. This is the function of the newly established World Climate Data Programme (see Section IV.4). A closely related program is the World Climate Applications Programme (WMO, 1980). Together these new international programs should improve the availability and application of climate data for planning and operations in many countries that lack the expertise or the computers needed to use our knowledge of climate and its influence on human activities. While the immediate thrust of this effort is to cope with short term climate variability, it will also help people prepare for long term climate change.

- *Provide public information and education.*  Disseminating the results of carbon dioxide/climate studies to reporters, environmentalists and other interested groups should raise the general level of public awareness about the problem. Such information would encourage the design of new products and facilities that could respond to new climatic conditions as well as to climatic variations. Furthermore, long term measures to cope with climate change will be more readily accepted if a well informed public understands the reasons for their adoption.

- *Transfer appropriate technology.*  Immediate investment in applied climatology and weather prediction techniques is highly desirable for most developing countries. These investments would fulfill needs in areas such as water supply, plant husbandry, energy resources, housing design, and land use planning (Sah, 1979; Lele, 1979). The benefits would likely outweigh the costs. As discussed in other sections, technology transfer should be encouraged in a number of areas, such as renewable energy resources and agrotechnology.

117

Again, even if there is no global climate change, there are benefits to be gained by implementing these and similar strategies. Thus, there is no need to delay action and wait for firmer scientific evidence about the carbon dioxide threat.

The need for vigorous initiatives throughout the world to cope with our growing population and changing environment has been voiced recently by the Council on Environmental Quality (CEQ, 1980). It states:

> The available evidence leaves no doubt that the world — including this nation — faces enormous, urgent, and complex problems in the decades immediately ahead. Prompt and vigorous changes in public policy around the world are needed to avoid or minimize these problems before they become unmanageable. Long lead times are required for effective action. If decisions are delayed until the problems became worse, options for effective action will be severely reduced.

Whether societies will have the required resources to take effective actions or adapt to major climate changes is another question. This will be determined by several indices. The first is gross national product (GNP), or income per capita. GNP is a rough measure of aggregate economic activity and is an index of the economic resources to build new facilities or move people.

The second is the gross rate of investment, or ratio of investment to GNP. A high ratio means that many new facilities are being built and capital stock is turning over rapidly. Since new plants and equipment can be designed for the expected climatic conditions and can be built in the right places, rapid turnover means that most of the capital stock can be tailored to a new economic or climatic regime.

The third measure is the flexibility and diversity of the capital stock. Some plants and equipment are so highly specialized that they cannot accommodate changes in raw materials, product design, or fuels. For example, an electricity generator can burn any two or all three of the fuels natural gas, oil, or coal. This greater flexibility means there is less need to replace the capital stock, making adjustment easier. Diversity of the capital stock gives the economy the resilience to avoid disaster in the face of changing conditions such as climate. This is much like diversifying crops, instead of depending on a monoculture. The monoculture can give greater yield under a narrow range of conditions but can lead to crop failure if conditions change. Hence, flexible, diverse capital stock may increase costs and lower output, but it offers insurance against changing conditions (see also Section III.1).

A fourth characteristic is the ability to foresee changing conditions and adapt to them quickly. A better educated population and good planning in social institutions will help. An important aspect of this is the ability and willingness of planners to recognize the signals of coming change and interpret them for the population and for the social institutions that lack this ability.

## 4.  International Institutions and Legal Mechanisms

Before we discuss the scope of likely international involvement in the carbon dioxide/climate problem we will briefly outline the background of international cooperation in studying and dealing with more general environmental questions.

### 4.1  History of organizations for environmental cooperation

Since the earliest voyages of exploration to the present there has been a desire to exchange information about our planet: the weather conditions, ocean currents, and other aspects. In 1873, at the suggestion of a group of sea captains, several nations agreed to form an international organization to link their fledgling weather services. This was the International Meteorological Organization (IMO), and its initial function was to standardize the measurements of weather and ocean conditions and to ensure that they were available for climatological studies (Nyberg, 1973).

In those days climatology was largely devoted to description of the existing climates of various regions. As early as 1900 there was a hint that fossil fuel burning could be a factor in global climate change (Chamberlain, 1899; Arrhenius, 1903) but these suggestions received little attention until some 50 years later. In the early part of this century climate was considered an unchanging part of the environment; people expected next year's weather and its variations to behave the same as in the past.

When the United Nations was created, after World War II, the IMO became one of its specialized agencies in 1951, calling itself the World Meteorological Organization. Included in its goals, as stated in the WMO Convention (1977), are:

- To facilitate worldwide cooperation in the establishment of networks of stations for making meteorological observations as well as hydrological and other physical observations related to meteorology, and to promote the establishment and maintenance of centers charged with the provision of meteorological and related services;
- To promote standardization of meteorological and related observations and to ensure the uniform publication of

observations and statistics;
- To further the application of meteorology to aviation, shipping, water problems, agriculture, and other human activities.

International cooperation between the world's weather services had become essential in the age of aviation. Weather observations were radioed around the world twice a day for making better forecasts. With satellites available in 1963 to help in both weather observations and long range communication, the WMO instituted an improved system to exchange information rapidly and systematically. It is called the World Weather Watch (WWW). Again, the emphasis was on making better weather forecasts, largely to satisfy the needs of aviation. Climatology was given secondary importance by the WMO.

However, the 1960s was also a period of heightened concern for the environment of the Earth; many feared that people could pollute the air and water and even alter the climate. Some sort of international action was needed. But the WMO and other international agencies were not in a position to take such action, so the United Nations decided to organize the Conference on the Human Environment in June 1972. The United Nations Environment Programme was then established to help develop programs designed to protect and improve the environment. The major tasks of UNEP are to (Wallén, 1978):
- Disseminate information on major environmental problems and the efforts being made to respond to them, in order to identify gaps, set objectives, and establish priorities;
- Formulate programs for action by the United Nations system or by other international organizations;
- Undertake those tasks recommended by the Environmental Fund.

In order to facilitate these goals, UNEP has set up the Global Environmental Monitoring System (GEMS), an environmental monitoring and assessment program. GEMS' objectives include (Martin and Sella, 1977):
- Expanding a warning system of threats to human health;
- Assessing global atmospheric pollution and its impact on climate;
- Assessing critical problems arising from agricultural and land use practices;
- Improving an international warning system of natural disasters.

120

It became clear to the WMO and its 140 weather service members that our knowledge and application of climate information would have to be improved. In February 1979 the WMO held the first World Climate Conference, which was titled: A Conference of Experts on Climate and Mankind (WMO, 1979). A major portion of the papers at this conference dealt with the various ways in which climate affects human activities and institutions.

One of the functions of the World Climate Conference was to approve plans for a new World Climate Programme (WCP), which it did. This program was subsequently approved by the WMO Congress in May, 1979, and became an official program at the beginning of 1980. The WCP has four component programs: Climate Data Programme; Climate Applications Programme; Climate Research Programme; and the Climate Impact Studies Programme. The WMO invited UNEP to take the primary responsibility for the Climate Impact Studies Programme, and UNEP's Governing Council accepted, though this component program remains under the aegis of the World Climate Programme.

The names of the four component programs are fairly self–explanatory. The Climate Data Programme is responsible for better acquisition and archiving of climate related data of all kinds. The Climate Applications Programme is designed to help developing countries make better use of climate information. The Climate Research Programme is devoted to a better understanding of the physical basis for climate variability and change, and is a continuation of the highly successful Global Atmospheric Research Programme (GARP). The responsibility for the Climate Research Programme is shared by the WMO and the International Council of Scientific Unions (ICSU). The Climate Impact Studies Programme will take on tasks outlined elsewhere in this report; it is the least well defined program at this time.

Thus, the scope and functions of those intergovernmental meteorological and environmental agencies have been officially established. The *nongovernmental* Scientific Committee on Problems of the Environment (SCOPE), a special ICSU committee, has broadened the institutional framework. Founded in 1969, SCOPE currently represents 23 member countries. In addition to focusing on the environmental needs of developing countries, SCOPE has launched a long term study of biogeochemical cycles of carbon, nitrogen, phosphorous and sulfur. The purpose of this project "is to provide decision makers at the global, regional, and national level with appropriate scientific knowledge for developing practical strategies for optimizing man's interaction with the carbon cycle" (Malone, 1978).

Since the end of the 1960s the growth of organizations and international meetings has accelerated, as have the plans for scientific and political cooperation. In 1972 the International Institute for Applied Systems Analysis (IIASA) was established as another nongovernmental organization. IIASA's membership consists of scientific academies throughout the world; presently 17 countries are represented. Its principal areas of research include resources and environment, human settlements and services, management and technology, and "system and decision sciences." "A concern for society's interaction with the climate pervades the Institute's entire research activity, both actually and latently" (Levien, 1978).

We should also mention the regional organizations gaining influence. Environmental activities of several of these are discussed in Section 4.3. It is notable that the Council of the European Communities (CEC) has approved and funded a European Climate Programme that has many similarities to the U.S. National Climate Program.

## 4.2 International legal mechanisms

We should not expect too much of international law when it comes to resolving cases that deal with injuries or damages caused by carbon dioxide-induced atmospheric warming. Ultimately, countries are free to comply with or ignore international law. In any case, there is currently no mechanism by which to set carbon dioxide standards, establish universally applied control measures, and enforce the so-called "global right to a clean atmosphere."

Obviously there is no policing body to control carbon dioxide production on a global scale, and there is little chance that one could be established in the foreseeable future (Meyer–Abich, 1980; Kellogg and Mead, 1977). It would make sense, however, to encourage international mechanisms that could:

- Examine the likely effects of a carbon dioxide-induced warming on national and international activities. Perhaps the Climate Impact Studies Programme under UNEP and WMO will be able to do this;
- Determine an equitable distribution of fossil fuel resources between countries;
- Recommend to governments, as far as practical, measures to deter activities that enhance the atmospheric burden of

carbon dioxide, such as "excessive" use of fossil fuel or large scale deforestation;

● Warn of impending climate related disasters, such as regional crop failures. One way to do this would be to continuously update forecasts of crop yields and inventories of food reserves;

● Exchange information on climate change and its impacts. Again, the Climate Impact Studies Programme may be in a position to do this.

Liability claims, sanctions, and indemnity awards may be awkward ways to resolve carbon dioxide related problems such as disruptions in trade, environmental damages, and population relocations. By the time such actions are brought to court, settled, and (if possible) enforced by future international legal mechanism, the potentially irreversible impacts will have probably already occurred. In the following three sections we will discuss some mechanisms of international law that could become applicable to carbon dioxide related issues in the next few decades.

### 4.3   International agreements

So far no international legal agreements or regulations have been used to resolve problems associated with increased atmospheric carbon dioxide. However, two recent international agreements may be moving in the right direction. First, the Organization for Economic Cooperation and Development (OECD) Environmental Committee has given some attention to the consequences of increased carbon dioxide emissions from coal production. In 1979, the Council on Coal and the Environment specifically recommended that: "Member countries, in the light of appropriate research results, seek to define acceptable fuel qualities, emissions levels or ambient media qualities, as appropriate, for carbon dioxide" (Weiss, 1980). Second, the European Commission for Europe in 1979 signed a "Convention on Transboundary Air Pollution." The 34 member states, including the U.S. and Canada, pledged "to limit, and as far as possible, gradually reduce and prevent air pollution." However, as Rosencrantz (1980) notes:

> . . . the agreement does not compel abatement action. It includes no mechanism for enforcement of its terms, nor does it delineate the responsibility of member states to abate pollution–causing damage in another state or to award compensation for such damage.

There are other types of treaties and conventions being negotiated that apply principles of international law to established areas of transnational significance, such as marine pollution, nuclear weapons tests, exploitation of the Antarctic, and the use of outer space. Nations engaging in these agreements have taken preliminary steps toward clarifying the mechanisms and procedures through which regulation, control, and enforcement policies can be implemented.

For example, the U.S. is proposing a treaty that would require signatory governments to prepare an International Environmental Impact Statement on major projects, such as building a large power plant or seeding clouds to enhance precipitation. Such projects could have adverse environmental effects on neighboring countries. As spelled out in the U.S. Senate Resolution 49 (Pell, 1977) the treaty would apply to potentially harmful activities affecting land, water, and atmospheric resources.

There seems to be a growing acceptance by nations of regional organizations such as the European Economic Community, the OECD, the Association of Southeast Asian Nations, and the Latin America Free Trade Association, among others. These groups are set up to deal with specific supranational problems. They may have a potentially valuable function in organizing cooperative plans of action for carbon dioxide control strategies, and for compensating member countries for damages resulting from climate change.

However, as we have already stressed, individual nations or even regional organizations cannot by themselves effectively reduce the buildup of atmospheric carbon dioxide. The problem is a global one so that all countries of the world must work together to limit use of fossil fuels and the resulting emissions.

## 4.4 International commissions

The findings and recommendations of international commissions, ranging from "conciliation commissions" to "arbitral tribunals" to "commissions of inquiry" can sometimes influence international behavior. The International Joint Commission set up by the United States and Canada was a particularly useful commission for investigating atmospheric pollution, recommending control measures, and supervising compliance with the provisions. For carbon dioxide problems, such commissions may be useful *ad hoc* devices to either arbitrate disputes or to establish the opinion of experts on controversial legal, political and scientific issues.

## 4.5 International conferences

Conducting international relations through special conferences is becoming an accepted practice among countries. The United Nations has encouraged this, convening such conferences as the Conference on the Human Environment, the Law of the Sea, the Law of Treaties, and Science and Technology for Development.

The value of recommendations of international conferences is that they tend to clarify general principles by calling attention to matters that *should* be dealt with within the domestic jurisdiction of member States. For instance, Recommendation 70 of the United Nations Conference on the Human Environment (1972) states:

> ... that Governments be mindful of activities in which there is an appreciable risk of effects on climate and to this end: a) Carefully evaluate the likelihood and magnitude of climatic effects and disseminate their findings to the maximum extent feasible before embarking on such activities; b) Consult fully other interested States when activities carrying a risk of such effects are being contemplated or implemented.

To date, the World Climate Conference, organized by the WMO and held in Geneva in 1979, has been the largest international effort to foresee and investigate potential human induced climatic changes.

We have only dealt with a few of the possible international legal mechanisms for handling the political and economic consequences of a global carbon dioxide–induced climatic change. Special mention should be made of diplomatic negotiations, the Permanent Court of Arbitration, and the International Court of Justice (Nanda, 1975; Weiss, 1978). Each of these institutional arrangements and procedures may be used to resolve possible carbon dioxide related damage and compensation disputes. It seems unlikely, however, that they could be effective in achieving worldwide action to reduce fossil fuel use.

## 5. Ethical Considerations

Different conceptions of "fairness," based on philosophical, legal, and economic principles will undoubtedly influence the behavior of governments when it comes to developing national and international alternative strategies for dealing with the impacts of a carbon dioxide–induced global warming. We explore here some of the more general ethical considerations.

## 5.1 Assessing responsibility

Inevitably, questions will arise concerning responsibility for the costs of the adverse climatic impacts that might be suffered by regions or nations as a consequence of increased atmospheric carbon dioxide. In practice this means that nations would need to agree on measures to determine the proportional indemnity to be charged to each region or country.

One measure that has been used to quantify the relative contribution of atmospheric carbon dioxide emissions from regions and countries, including developed* and developing** nations, has emphasized emissions in single, specific years (Rotty, 1978; Rotty, 1979b; Rotty and Marland, 1980; Perry and Landsberg, 1977). In our view, responsibility for carbon dioxide emissions should be calculated in terms of cumulative emissions. This point is elaborated below.

In order to compute the future atmospheric burden of carbon dioxide, based on scenarios of future fossil fuel use and past emissions, one must use a model of the carbon cycle that accurately reflects the transient response of the Earth–atmosphere–ocean system to global carbon dioxide inputs (see Section II.2). For example, the model of Siegenthaler and Oeschger (1978), provides a way to calculate the response of the system to a "pulse" input of carbon dioxide. Those authors point out the limitations of their model in dealing with large future inputs of carbon dioxide to the atmosphere, since the transient response is a function of changes induced in the chemistry or dynamics of the ocean. However, their model provides results that can be used to approximate the date at which the atmospheric burden of carbon dioxide will have reached a specific level, that is, double the assumed "preindustrial" value of 290 ppmv. This model can also be used to calculate the relative contribution of developed and developing countries.

The first step in the application of Siegenthaler and Oeschger's model is to determine the fraction of each year's emission of carbon (as carbon dioxide) that remains airborne after being released. The complete calculation requires a sum of the following kind:

$$\sum_{t = 1860}^{T} f(T - t)\, E(t)$$

---

\* Australia, Canada, Japan, Israel, South Africa, United States, Western Europe, Eastern Europe, Soviet Union.

\*\* Africa (other than South Africa), Caribbean America, Middle East (including Turkey), Far East, Oceania, China, Democratic People's Republic of Korea, Viet Nam.

which gives the cumulative carbon burden, at time T, that results from emissions characterized by an annual rate E(t) if a fraction, f, remains of each year's emissions after T–t years. Siegenthaler and Oeschger's decay factor, f(t), can be parameterized as x/x+t with x=40, which takes account of the slow absorption of the additional carbon dioxide by the deep ocean water and the biosphere. For example, the remaining fraction of the 1970 emissions will be 50 percent in 2010, but only 40 percent of the 1950 emissions will remain airborne in 2010.

The carbon dioxide doubling date and the relative fraction of the added carbon dioxide contributed by developed and developing countries were computed by using the historical record of emissions for the period 1860–1976 (Zimen et al., 1977; United Nations, 1979), as given in Appendix A, and various scenarios of future carbon dioxide release that assume an exponential growth of E(t) after 1976. By evaluating the sum above, estimates are obtained of the growth in the atmospheric burden of carbon dioxide as well as the date at which the doubling will occur.

Figure IV.3 illustrates the fraction of the doubled airborne carbon dioxide contributed by developed and developing nations, as well as the date when the doubling will occur. The annual growth rates range from 0.01 to 0.04 per year (approximately 1 to 4 percent per year) for developed nations, and 0.01 to 0.08 per year for developing nations (approximately 1 to 8 percent per year).

For the developing nations to exceed 50 percent of the contribution to doubled airborne carbon dioxide in the first half of the next century, they must maintain an average annual growth rate in fossil fuel use that exceeds 0.06 if the developed nations have only a 0.02 growth rate, or 0.04 if the latter can hold growth rates down to 0.01. Although developing nations have exceeded these levels in the past, such growth rates may become increasingly difficult for the Third World to maintain, given their economic prospects for 1980 and beyond (Abbott, 1979; GATT, 1979). Nor is it certain that the developed nations can limit their growth rates of fossil fuel use to less than 0.02 (Marshall, 1980).

Indeed, a growth rate well below previous estimates (Rotty, 1978; Rotty, 1979a; Perry and Landsberg, 1977) would seem more likely in the case of the Third World. Direct and indirect financial subsidies from OPEC have enabled the 89 oil importing developing countries to better cope with world inflation, sharp increases in the price of oil, and the heavy burden of meeting external debts owed to developed countries (Attiga, 1979). Given the possibly imminent

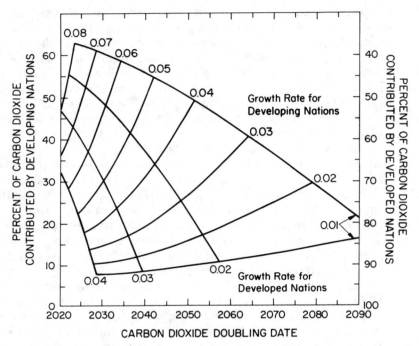

**Figure IV.3.** Percent of the doubled airborne carbon dioxide contributed by developed and developing nations. Note that growth rates are used in an exponential carbon dioxide release model for dates after 1976 (Schware and Friedman, 1980).

depletion of OPEC's oil supply, no one can be certain how much longer this aid will be available.

The oil importing developing countries face substantial energy problems, even if their economic ties with OPEC countries continue. There is also no guarantee that as petroleum resources are depleted and replaced by coal, the developing nations will have the wherewithal to buy it from the coal–rich nations of China, the U.S.S.R., and the U.S. At the same time, very large investments in either oil or coal imports will diminish developing countries' ability to invest in agricultural modernization and industrial development.

Hence, if global fossil fuel growth rates slow to 0.01 and 0.02 for developed and developing countries respectively, the carbon dioxide doubling would occur in 2080, and 70 percent of the carbon dioxide airborne at that date will have been contributed by

128

developed nations (see Figure IV.3). If this occurs, Third World contributions to global carbon dioxide emissions may be considerably less than expected.

A less likely continued high growth scenario, in which the growth rates of the 1970s persist (see Appendix A), shows fossil fuel growth rates of 0.03 and 0.07 in developed and developing countries, respectively. In this case, the carbon dioxide doubling will occur before 2025 and 58 percent of it will be contributed by developed nations.

In conclusion, if the international community is ever to assess responsibility for carbon dioxide production and altered climate, calculations must encompass a range of past as well as future scenarios of fossil fuel use and the resulting carbon dioxide emissions. Our preliminary calculations indicate that, through the next century, developed countries might have to bear much of the responsibility for new climatic regimes; they are the suppliers of fuel to the world, the major consumers, and the major cumulative contributors of carbon dioxide to the atmosphere.

## 5.2  The polluter pays principle

The OECD has concluded that, when it comes to environmental matters, national borders have no meaning. Hence, the Council adopted the Polluter Pays Principle (PPP) to deal with pollution that crosses state boundaries. Most OECD member countries have included the PPP in their domestic legislation. As the OECD recommended in 1972, the PPP is:

> ... to be used for allocating costs of pollution prevention and control measures to encourage rational use of scarce environmental resources and to avoid distortions in international trade and investment ... This principle means that the polluter should bear the expenses of carrying out the above-mentioned measures decided by public authorities to ensure that the environment is in an acceptable state. In other words, the cost of these measures should be reflected in the cost of goods and services which cause pollution in production and/or consumption.

The underlying assumption of the PPP is this: The precise social costs to be exacted from the international community by an environmental problem such as pollution cannot be ascertained. Hence, it is more practical to require discharging countries to pay for *pollution control* rather than the environmental damages they may cause. However, some point out that assigning partial liability —

that is, control costs and not residual damages — to environmental offenders is a limited principle of equity and economic efficiency (Ruff, 1976; d'Arge, 1976; Barde, 1976).

Environmental damage funds may be another way to compensate parties for injuries resulting from increased levels of atmospheric carbon dioxide. Such funds may be applicable to impacts on health and disease (see Section III.7) and agricultural productivity (see Section III.3). The Dutch Air Pollution Fund and the Japanese Law for the Compensation of Pollution Related Health Damage are two examples of national programs based on this principle (Rosencrantz, 1980). Establishing international funds to compensate for carbon dioxide–induced environmental damages should be considered. But determining who should compensate injured parties internationally is complicated by uncertainties about each nation's relative contributions to the total atmospheric carbon dioxide emissions, as shown in the previous section.

### 5.3 Efforts to assist developing countries

Developed nations might help developing countries in two important areas: researching climate related problems peculiar to developing countries; and constructing self reliant, energy efficient nonfossil fuel technologies that are relatively risk free.

Applying climate knowledge to socioeconomic activities is of fundamental and immediate importance to developing countries. As the World Climate Conference (WMO, 1979) recently noted, there are needs for:

- Broadly qualified climatologists knowledgeable in applications areas who can interpret user needs in climatological terms and assist users in employing climatic information in their planning and decision processes;
- Specialists from other disciplines, such as agriculture, hydrology or marine activities with an appreciable knowledge of climatology;
- Data specialists who can transform existing archives of general purpose data into special purpose information for specific applications;
- Technicians to apply computer and other modern technologies to these tasks.

The Climate Data Programme and the Climate Applications Programme of the WCP are designed to satisfy these needs (see Section 4.1).

Too often, technologies inappropriate to conditions in developing countries are offered them. A study by the United Nations Conference on Trade and Development (UNCTAD, 1972) notes that:

> The imported technology may be inappropriate because it makes use of relatively scarce factors of production (e.g., foreign exchange) and leaves abundant factors idle (e.g., labor); or because it ignores the implications of the output (e.g., luxury products); or of the nature of social organization (e.g., the inequal distribution of income) which it helps to perpetuate.

Investigating the ecological costs of introducing various technologies to developing countries, the Conference on the Ecological Aspects of International Development (Farvar and Milton, 1972) concluded that:

> Little concern had ever been given to anticipating ecological costs and side effects, to say nothing of having such factors serve as inputs to decision making in development projects. In example after example, we found that large dams, irrigation projects, oil and mineral developments, industrial plants, nomadic settlement efforts, resettlement programs . . . food distribution efforts . . . and programs to build fossil fuel and atomic energy plants were being promoted through the world with little or no attention to their environmental consequences.

Lovins (1977) has reviewed the rapid modernization process at work in developing countries, including unchecked deforestation, increased burning of fossil fuels, and the breaking of relations with colonial countries. He notes that perhaps the most effective and practical contribution developed countries can make is to produce for export (and use domestically) "soft" energy technologies.

> Though neither glamorous nor militarily useful, these technologies are socially effective — especially in poor countries that need such scale, versatility and simplicity even more than rich countries do . . . Soft technologies do not carry with them inappropriate cultural patterns or values; they capitalize on poor countries' most abundant resources (including such protein poor plants as cassava, eminently suited to making fuel alcohols), helping to redress the severe energy imbalance between temperate and tropical regions, they can often be made locally from local materials and do not require dependence and commercial monopoly; they conform to modern concepts of agriculturally based

ecodevelopment from the bottom up, particularly in the rural villages.

In practice, initiatives to help Third World countries develop climatological, educational and training opportunities, and apply appropriate energy technologies would permit a graduated response to the carbon dioxide problem. Moreover, these steps would have economic and social benefits independent of a carbon dioxide–induced climate change, as stressed in Section 3.

## 5.4 The "Right to Food"

In 1948 the United Nations Declaration of Universal Rights proclaimed that "everyone has the right to a standard of living adequate for the health and well–being of himself and his family, including food, housing, and medical care." This universal "right to food" has become a standard for formulating national and international duties and guarantees. More recently, the U.S. Congress passed a resolution in 1976 stating that "every person in this country and throughout the world has the right to food — the right to a nutritionally adequate diet — and that this right is henceforth to be recognized as a cornerstone of United States policy." These declarations, and others like them such as the 1974 Report of the World Food Conference, may acquire new meaning with the prospect of reduced food supplies and climate shifts induced by a global warming.

Obviously, production and distribution of enough food to meet basic nutritional needs cannot be ensured by merely proclaiming it as a moral right. World hunger and malnutrition are a result of economic and political structures that disrupt these activities. These structures, along with likely population increases, will have to be dealt with if the world's food problem is to be solved in the coming years (Christensen, 1978; Garcia, 1980).

## 5.5 The "Right to a Clean Atmosphere"

In referring to the carbon dioxide problem, this concept means: The atmosphere cannot be owned and therefore should be managed collectively for the common good of all countries and individuals (Kellogg and Mead, 1977); and the atmosphere was originally free from an excess burden of carbon dioxide so the right to emit the gas is subject to negotiation. Even though such negotiation has never occurred, there are international laws and principles that may make "harmful" carbon dioxide emissions illegal.

In 1972 the United Nations Conference on the Human Environment held in Stockholm adopted the first steps toward legal and political accountability in global environmental matters. Principle 21 of the Declaration makes States responsible " ... to ensure that activities within their jurisdiction or control do not cause damage to the environment of other States or of areas beyond the limits of national jurisdiction." Principle 22 provides that:

> States shall cooperate to develop further the international law regarding liability and compensation for the victims of pollution and other environmental damage caused by activities within the jurisdiction or control of said States to areas beyond that jurisdiction.

The 1971 United Nations resolutions on Development and Environment also dealt with the question of the right of all people to a clean environment, as did the much earlier and more limited Council of the OECD Convention (Article 2, 1960), which stated that:

> . . . the members agree that they will, both individually and jointly . . . pursue policies designed . . . to avoid developments which might endanger their economies or those of other countries.

Of course, there are formidable problems in enforcing such international principles. For one thing, the Convention does not define standards (or even how to set them) for emissions or general environmental quality. Hence, to a large extent these principles just serve as voluntary guidelines for member countries.

# REFERENCES

Abbott, G.C., 1979: *International Indebtedness and the Developing Countries.* Croom Helm, London.

Arrhenius, S., 1903: *Lehrbuch der kosmischen Physik* 2, Hirzel, Leipzig.

Attiga, A.A, 1979: Global energy transition and the third world. Third World Foundation, London.

Baes, C.F., Jr., S.E. Beall, D.W. Lee and G. Marland, 1980: The collection, disposal, and storage of carbon dioxide. In *Interactions of Energy and Climate,* W. Bach, J. Pankrath, and J. Williams (eds.), Reidel, Dordrecht, Holland, 495–520.

Baird, A., 1975: Towards an explanation of disaster proneness. University of Bradford, Disaster Research Unit Occasional Paper No. 10, Bradford, England.

Barde, J.P., 1976: National and international policy alternatives for environmental control and their economic implications. In *Studies in International Environmental Economics,* I. Walter (ed.), Wiley, New York, 137–157.

Burton, I., R.W. Kates, and G.F. White, 1978: *The Environment As Hazard.* Oxford University Press, Oxford.

Carter, V.G., and T. Dale, 1974: *Topsoil and Civilization* (revised edition). University of Oklahoma Press, Norman, Okla.

C.E.Q., 1979: *Environmental Quality.* The tenth annual report of the Council on Environmental Quality, U.S. Gov't Printing Office, 041–011–00047–5, Washington, D.C.

C.E.Q., 1980: *The Global 2000 Report to the President,* Vol. 1. Report by Council on Environmental Quality and the Department of State, G.O. Barney (Study Dir.), Washington, D.C.

Chamberlain, T.C., 1899: An attempt to frame a working hypothesis of the cause of glacial epochs on an atmospheric basis. *J. Geology,* 7.

Christensen, U., 1978: The right to food: How to guarantee. *Alternatives* IV,2, 181–220.

Cooper, C., 1978: What might man–induced climate change mean? *Foreign Affairs* 56,3, 500–520.

d'Arge, R.C., 1976: Transfrontier pollution: Some issues on regulation. In *Studies in International Environmental Economics,* I. Walter (ed.), Wiley, New York, 257–278.

Daly, H.E., 1979: On thinking about future energy requirements. In *Sociopolitical Effects of Energy Use and Policy,* Report to the Sociopolitical Effects Resource Group Risk and Impact Panel, NRC, National Academy of Sciences, Washington, D.C.

Darmstadter, J.J., et al., 1977: How industrial societies use energy: A comparative analysis. Resources for the Future, Johns Hopkins University Press, Baltimore, Md.

Darmstadter, J., and S. Schurr, 1974: World energy resources and demand. *Phil. Trans. Roy. Soc. London A276,* No. 1261, 413.

Dyson, F. and G. Marland, 1979: Technical fixes for the climatic effects of $CO_2$. In *Workshop on the Global Effects of Carbon Dioxide from Fossil Fuels,* CONF–770385, U.S. Dept. of Energy, Washington, D.C., 111–118.

Farvar, M.T. and J.P. Milton, eds., 1972: *The Careless Technology: Ecology and International Development.* Natural History Press, New York.

Garcia, R., 1980: *Nature Pleads Not Guilty.* Pergamon Press, New York (in press).

GATT, 1979: International trade 1978–1979. General Agreement on Tariffs and Trade, Geneva.

Gibrat, R., 1978: Deep seas: Climate and economic development. In *Carbon Dioxide, Climate and Society,* J. Williams (ed.), Pergamon, New York, 291–299.

Glantz, 1977: *Desertification: Environmental Degradation in and around Arid Lands.* M.H. Glantz (ed.), Westview Press, Boulder, Colo.

Hewapathirane, D., 1977: Flood hazard in Sri Lanka: Human adjustments and alternatives. Ph.D. dissertation, Department of Geography, University of Colorado, Boulder, Colo.

Hitch, C.J., ed., 1978: Energy Conservation and Economic Growth. AAAS, Westview Press, Boulder, Colo.

Hoffert, M., Y.–C. Wey, A. Callegari and W. Broecker, 1979: Atmospheric response to deep–sea injections of fossil–fuel carbon dioxide. *Climatic Change 2,* 53–68.

Holdren, J., 1977: A strategy to buy time. *Bull. of the Atomic Scientists*, 33, 58–63.

Kates, R.W., 1962: Hazard and choice perception in flood plain management. Department of Geography, University of Chicago, Research Paper No. 78, Chicago.

Kates, R.W., 1980: Climate and society: Lessons from recent events. *Weather*, 35, 1, 17–25.

Kellogg, W.W. and M. Mead, (eds.), 1977: *The Atmosphere: Endangered and Endangering.* Fogarty Intl. Cntr. Proc. No. 39, Natl. Inst. of Health, Washington, D.C. (DHEW Publ. No. (NIH)77–1065).

Kovda, V.A. 1980: *Land Aridization and Drought Control.* Westview Press, Boulder, Colo.

Lele, U., 1979: *The Design of Rural Development: Lessons from Africa.* Johns Hopkins University Press, Baltimore.

Levien, R.E., 1978: Welcoming address. In *Carbon Dioxide, Climate and Society,* J. Willaims (ed.), Pergamon Press, New York.

Loomis, R.S., 1979: $CO_2$ and the biosphere. *Workshop on the Global Effects of Carbon Dioxide from Fossil Fuels.* W.P. Elliott and L. Machta (eds.), Miami Beach, Fla., 7–11, March, U.S. Dept of Energy, Washington, D.C. (CONF–770385).

Lovins, A.B., 1977: *Soft Energy Paths: Toward a Durable Peace.* Friends of the Earth, Ballinger, Cambridge, Mass.

Malone T.F., 1978: Introductory remarks from SCOPE. In *Carbon Dioxide, Climate and Society,* J. Williams (ed.), Pergamon Press, New York.

Marchetti, C., 1977: On geoengineering and the $CO_2$ problem. *Climatic Change* 1, 59–68.

Marchetti, C., 1979: Constructive solutions to the $CO_2$ problem. In *Man's Impact on Climate,* W. Bach, J. Pankrath and W. Kellogg (eds.), Elsevier, New York, 299–311.

Marshall, E. 1980: Energy forecasts: Sinking to new lows. *Science* 208, 1353–1356.

Martin, B. and F. Sella, 1977: The global environmental monitoring system. In *International Environmental Monitoring, A Bellagio Conference,* The Rockefeller Foundation, New York.

Mattei, F., 1979: Climate variability and agricultures in the semi-arid tropics. In *Proc. World Climate Conference*, WMO No. 537, World Meteorological Organization, Geneva, 475–509.

Meyer–Abich, K.M., 1980: Socioeconomic impacts of $CO_2$-induced climatic changes and the comparative chances of alternative political responses: Prevention, compensation, and adaptation. *Climatic Change*, 2, 373–386.

Mokyr, J., 1980: Industrialization and poverty in Ireland and the Netherlands. *J. Interdisciplinary History*, 10,3, 429–458.

Mustacchi, C., P. Armenante and V. Cena, 1978: Carbon dioxide disposal in the ocean. In *Carbon Dioxide, Climate and Society*, J. Williams (ed.), Pergamon, New York, 283–289.

NAS, 1979: Risks associated with nuclear power: A critical review of the literature. National Academy of Sciences, Washington, D.C.

NRC, 1979a: Alternative energy demand futures to 2010. In *Report of the Demand and Conservation Panel*, National Academy of Sciences, Washington, D.C.

NRC, 1979b: Energy in transition 1985–2010. In *Final Report of the Committee on Nuclear and Alternative Energy Systems*, National Academy of Sciences, Washington, D.C.

Nanda, V.P., 1975: The establishment of international standards for transnational environmental injury. *Iowa Law Review*, 60, 5, 1089–1127.

Nyberg, A., 1973: General review of the science of meteorology during the last 100 years. Lecture presented at the IMO/WMO Centenary Conferences, WMO No. 370, World Meteorological Organization, Geneva.

OECD, 1972: Recommendations of the Council on Guiding Principles Concerning International Economic Aspects of Environmental Policies. C(72)128, Organization for Economic Cooperation and Development, Paris, June 6.

OECD, 1978: OECD member countries, 1978. *OECD Observer* 91, 20–21.

Oguntoyinbo, J.A. and R.S. Odingo, 1979: Climatic variability and land use: An African perspective. In *Proceedings of the World Climate Conference*, WMO No. 537, World Meteorological Organization, Geneva, 552–580.

Pell, C., 1977: Senate resolution 49 relating to international environmental impact statements. *Congressional Record,* Washington, D.C., 123, 12 (January 24).

Perry, H. and Landsberg, H., 1977: Projected world energy consumption. In *Energy and Climate,* National Academy of Sciences, Washington, D.C., 35–50.

Pochin, E.E., 1976: Estimated population exposure from nuclear power production and other radiation sources. Organization for Economic Cooperation and Development (OECD), Paris.

Rabb, T.K., 1980: The effects of climatic change in the past. Social and Institutional Responses Working Group IV, American Association for the Advancement of Science Climate Project, Washington, D.C., draft paper.

Rosencrantz, A., 1980: The problem of transboundary pollution. *Environment,* 22,5, 15–20.

Rotty, R.M., 1978: The atmospheric $CO_2$ consequence of heavy dependence on coal. In *Carbon Dioxide, Climate and Society,* J. Williams (ed.), Pergamon Press, New York.

Rotty, R.M., 1979a: (Material presented before Congress). In *Carbon Dioxide Accumulation in the Atmosphere, Synthetic Fuels and Energy Policy — A Symposium,* Committee on Governmental Affairs, U.S. Senate, Washington, D.C., July, 185–194.

Rotty, R.M., 1979b: Energy demand and global climate change. In *Man's Impact on Climate,* W. Bach, J. Pankrath and W. Kellogg (eds.), Elsevier, New York, 269–283.

Rotty, R.M. and Marland, G., 1980: Constraints on carbon dioxide production from fossil fuel use. Report of the Institute for Energy Analysis, Res. Mem. ORAV/IEA–80–9, Oak Ridge, Tenn.

Ruff, L.E., 1976: The economics of transnational pollution. *Economics of Transfrontier Pollution,* Organization for Economic Cooperation and Development, Paris, 7–10.

Sagan, L.A., 1972: Human costs of nuclear power. *Science* 177, 487–493.

Sah, R., 1979: Priorities of LDCs in weather and climate. Unpublished paper, Economic Research Unit, University of Pennsylvania.

Sakamoto, C., N. Strommen and A. Yao, 1979: Assessment with agroclimatological information. *Climatic Change* 2, 7–20.

Schaake, J.C., Jr., and Z. Kaczmarek, 1979: Climate variability and the design and operation of water resource systems. In *Proc. World Climate Conference*, WMO No. 537, World Meteorological Organization, Geneva, 290–312.

Schipper, L., 1976: Raising the productivity of energy utilization. *Ann. Rev. Energy* 1, 455–517.

Schipper, L., and A. Lichtenberg, 1976: Efficient energy use and well being: The Swedish example. *Science* 194, 1001–1013.

Schneider, S.H. with L.E. Mesirow, 1976: *The Genesis Strategy*. Plenum, New York.

Schware, R. and E.J. Friedman, 1980: Anthropogenic climate change: Assessing the responsibility of developed and developing countries (in press).

Siegenthaler, U. and Oeschger, H., 1978: Predicting future atmospheric carbon dioxide levels. *Science* 199, 388–395.

Steinberg, M. and A. Albanese, 1980: Environmental control technology for atmospheric carbon dioxide. Presented at the International Workshop on Energy/Climate Interactions, Münster, F.R.G.

Stobaugh, R. and D. Yergin (eds.), 1979: *Energy Future*. Random House, New York.

Time, 1979: Schmoo tree: It gives food and fuel. *Time Magazine*, December 10, 95.

UNCTAD, 1972: Guidelines for the study of the transfer of technology to developing countries. United Nations Conference on Trade and Development, United Nations, New York.

United Nations, 1948: Universal Declaration of Human Rights. U.N. Document A/811, Article 25.1. United Nations, New York.

United Nations Conference on the Human Environment, 1972: Report of the United Nations Conference on the Human Environment. U.N. Doc. A/Conf. 48/14/Rev. 1. Stockholm, June.

United Nations, 1979: World energy supplies. Statistical papers, Series J, Department of International Economic and Social Affairs, Statistical Office, United Nations, New York.

U.S. Congress, 1976: The right–to–food resolution. Hearings before the Subcommittee on International Resources, Food and Energy,

94th Congress, 2nd Session, House Resolution 393. U.S. Government Printing Office, Washington, D.C.

Wallén, C.C., 1978: Statement on behalf of UNEP. In *Carbon Dioxide, Climate and Society,* J. Williams (ed.), Pergamon Press, New York.

Weiss, E.B., 1978: International liability for weather modification. *Climatic Change,* 1,3, 267–290.

Weiss, E.B., 1980: A resource management approach to $CO_2$ during the century of transition. Paper presented at the International Law, Institutions, and World Climate Change Workshop, University of Denver College of Law, Denver, Colo., July.

WMO, 1977: Effects of Human Activities on Global Climate. Technical Note No. 156, World Meteorological Organization, Geneva.

WMO, 1979: *Proceedings of the World Climate Conference.* WMO No. 537, World Meteorological Organization, Geneva.

WMO, 1980: *Outline Plan and Basis for the World Climate Programme 1980–1983.* WMO No. 540, World Meteorological Organization, Geneva.

Yao, A.Y.M., 1973: Evaluating climatic limitations for a specific agricultural enterprise. *Agricultural Meteorol.* 12, 65–73.

Zimen, K.E., P. Offermann and G. Hartmann, 1977: Source functions of $CO_2$ and the future $CO_2$ burden in the atmosphere. *Zeits. Naturforschung* 32a, 1544–1554.

# APPENDICES

## APPENDIX A

## PAST AND FUTURE FOSSIL FUEL CONSUMPTION AND CARBON DIOXIDE EMISSIONS

### 1. Past Energy Use and Attempts to Predict It

Considerable uncertainty surrounds estimates of past and future fossil fuel consumption and the resulting carbon dioxide emissions. The fact that scientists disagree about future energy consumption and emissions is not surprising. But it means that developing the required economic, demographic, and energy scenarios will be a challenge. However, it is also troubling that even estimates of past energy consumption and emissions differ, despite the available data.

For example, Darmstadter and Schurr (1974) have compared energy use projections for the 1960s with the actual annual energy growth rate for the entire world, and for Western Europe, the United States, and Japan in particular. These data reveal a consistent underestimation of energy growth, especially for world oil consumption and U.S. oil imports. The discrepancies between projected and actual energy consumption for the 1960s are shown in Table A.1.

It is also interesting to compare energy growth in the 1970s with the projections in Table A.1. We can see that these expectations were consistently high, by no less than 1.6 percent globally and 1.8 percent for the U.S. — apparently few of the experts foresaw the reductions in growth rates that occurred between these two decades. Thus, major errors in projections of the past have included both large underestimates and overestimates. It also seems that misleading conclusions can result if we assume that the range of independent estimates of future fuel use will include the actual value, since large systematic errors have been common in the past.

Many of the discrepancies in the emission estimates result from uncertainties about the quantity of carbon dioxide produced from burning a given quantity of fossil fuel. For example, Keeling (1973) and Rotty (1973) compute the carbon released using a "carbon dioxide factor." This factor is derived from information on the carbon content of

**Table A.1.** Review of past energy consumption projections (Adapted from Darmstadter and Schurr, 1974).

| Region | Actual Data — Period | Actual Data — Average Annual Growth Rate (%) | Projections — Reference* | Projections — Period | Projections — Average Annual Growth Rate (%) |
|---|---|---|---|---|---|
| World | 1960–70 | 5.6 | (A) | 1960–70 | 4.6 |
|  | 1970–78 | 3.2 | (G) | 1970–80 | 4.8 |
|  |  |  | (B) | 1960–80 | 5.0 |
| Western Europe | 1960–70 | 6.3 | (C) | 1955–75 | 2.8 |
|  |  |  | (A) | 1960–70 | 4.4 |
|  |  |  | (A) | 1970–80 | 4.0 |
|  |  |  | (B) | 1964–70 | 4.2 |
|  |  |  | (B) | 1970–80 | 4.1 |
| United States | 1960–70 | 4.2 | (D) | 1960–70 | 2.9 |
|  | 1973–79 | 1.0 | (G) | 1970–80 | 2.8 |
|  |  |  | (A) | 1960–70 | 3.6 |
|  |  |  | (A) | 1970–80 | 3.3 |
| Japan | 1960–70 | 11.9 | (A) | 1960–70 | 9.1 |
|  |  |  | (A) | 1970–80 | 7.0 |
|  |  |  | (B) | 1964–70 | 10.0 |
|  |  |  | (B) | 1970–80 | 6.9 |
| **Oil Consumption** |  |  |  |  |  |
| Western Europe | 1962–72 | 10.5 | (B) | 1964–80 | 4.1 |
| United States | 1962–72 | 4.6 | (A) | 1960–70 | 3.5 |
|  |  |  | (A) | 1970–80 | 2.7 |
|  |  |  | (E) | 1965–75 | 3.4 |
|  |  |  | (E) | 1975–80 | 2.9 |
|  |  |  | (F) | 1965–80 | 3.1 |
| Japan | 1962–72 | 17.5 | (B) | 1964–70 | 14.3 |
|  |  |  | (B) | 1970–80 | 8.3 |

*Symbols refer to the following references:
(A) European Coal and Steel Community, 1966: *Review of the Long Term Energy Outlook of the European Community*, Luxembourg;
(B) O.E.C.D., 1966: *Energy Policy*, Paris;
(C) O.E.E.C., 1960: *Towards a New Energy Pattern in Europe*, Brussels;
(D) Landsberg, H., L.L. Fischman and J.L. Fisher, 1963: *Resources in America's Future. Resources for the Future*, Johns Hopkins, Baltimore;
(E) Schurr, S.H., P.T. Homan, et al., 1971: *Middle Eastern Oil and the Western World: Prospects and Problems*. Elsevier, New York;
(F) U.S. Department of the Interior, 1968: *United States Petroleum through 1980*. U.S. Department of the Interior, Washington, D.C.;
(G) U.S. Department of Energy, 1980: *Monthly Energy Review* (May), U.S. Department of Energy, Washington, D.C.

the fuel and the fraction oxidized to carbon dioxide when it is burned. Multiplying the factor times the mass (or in the case of natural gas, the volume) of fuel used gives a measure of the carbon released.

Other authors, such as Perry and Landsberg (1977), Steinberg et al., (1978), Woodwell et al., (1979) and Rotty (1979b) convert energy content of the fuel directly to carbon emission. Zimen et al., (1977) have chosen to present these data in terms of moles of carbon dioxide released. (There are 12.011 grams of carbon per mole of carbon dioxide.) Niehaus (1976) provides data on the tons of carbon dioxide released for each ton of "coal equivalent" used. Table A.2 summarizes the conversions used by various authors and presents the data in terms of carbon released per terrawatt–year ($10^{12}$ watt–years) of energy used.

We must also consider how carbon dioxide levels will be affected when one energy source is substituted for another. Figure A.1 illustrates the possibilities. For example, if coal is replaced by natural gas, carbon emissions would be decreased by $0.33 \times 10^9$ tons for each terrawatt–year. On the other hand, replacing coal with synthetic gas derived from coal increases emissions by $0.27 - 0.51 \times 10^9$ tons of carbon per terrawatt–year.

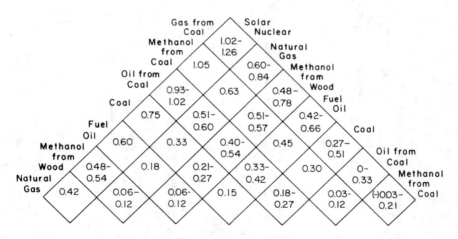

**Figure A.1.** Change in carbon emission for a given substitution of energy source. Replacing the source on the left with the one on the right decreases emission by the amount indicated (expressed in units of $10^{15}$ grams of carbon per terrawatt–year of energy used). Reversing the substitution process increases emissions (prepared by E. Friedman).

**Table A.2.  Carbon release per terrawatt-year ($10^9$ tons).**

| | Zimen et al. (1977) | Keeling (1973) | Perry & Landsberg (1977) | Rotty (1979a) | Steinberg et al. (1978) | Woodwell et al. (1979) | Niehaus (1976) | Rotty (1978) |
|---|---|---|---|---|---|---|---|---|
| Coal | | 0.759 | | | | 0.747 | | 0.759 |
| Lignite | | 1.546 | | | | | 1.010 | |
| Coal and Lignite | | | 0.767 | | | | | |
| Crude Petroleum | 0.771 | 0.529 | | | | | 0.654 | 0.568-0.649 |
| Natural Gas Liquids | 0.647 | | | | | | | |
| Natural Gas | 0.430 | 0.436 | 0.439 | | 0.406 | 0.433 | 0.562 | 0.430 |
| Coke | | | | | 0.962 | | | |
| Bituminous Coal | | | | | 0.795 | | 0.822 | |
| Wood and Cellulose | | | | | 0.667 | | | |
| Gasoline and Fuel Oil | | | 0.613 | | 0.547 | 0.598 | | |
| Hydrogen | | | | | | | | |
| –natural gas reforming | | | | | 0.406 | | | |
| –geothermal electrolytic | | | | | 0.149 | | | |
| –solar electrolytic | | | | | 0.0 | | | |
| –nuclear electrolytic | | | | | 0.0 | | | |
| Natural plus flared gas | 0.497 | | | | | | | |
| Methane (natural) | | | | | | | 0.487 | |
| –autothermal[1] | | | | | | | 1.205 | |
| –allothermal[2] | | | | | | | 0.876 | |
| Benzine | | | | | 0.702 | | | |
| Cement | 0.137 | 0.1373 | (see notes) | | | | | |

144

Table A.2. (Continued)

| | Zimen et al. (1977) | Keeling (1973) | Perry & Landsberg (1977) | Rotty (1979a) | Steinberg et al. (1978) | Woodwell et al. (1979) | Niehaus (1976) | Rotty (1978) |
|---|---|---|---|---|---|---|---|---|
| Synthetics | | | | | | | | |
| —natural gas from coal | | | | | 1.258 | 1.016 | | |
| —methanol from coal | | | | | 1.037 | | | |
| —hydrogen from coal | | | | | 0.995 | | | |
| —oil from coal | | | | 0.939 | | 1.016 | | 1.010 |
| —oil from shale | | | | 1.169 | | | | |
| —oil from crude | | | | 0.534 | | | | |
| —methanol from wood | | | | | 0.517 | | | 0.478–0.538 |

Note: All data are in units of $10^9$ tons of carbon release per terrawatt-year of energy used. For cement, $= 10^{15}$ BTU per $10^{10}$ tons of cement produced.

Conversions Used:  12.011 kg carbon $= 10^3$ mol $CO_2$

1 Quad  $= 23 \times 10^6$ tons oil, $= 27 \times 10^9$ m³ gas, $= 36.63 \times 10^6$ tons coal,
  $= 1.06 \times 10^{18}$ joules, $= 10^{15}$ BTU

1 ton carbon  $= 3.66$ tons $CO_2$

1 Quad/yr.  $= 4.76 \times 10^5$ barrels of oil per day

Coal has 2.25 the energy content of lignite.

[1] 1 ton of coal — 1030 Nm³ $CO_2$ + 700 Nm³ $CH_4$
[2] 1 ton of coal — 700 Nm³ $CO_2$ + 880 Nm³ $CH_4$

145

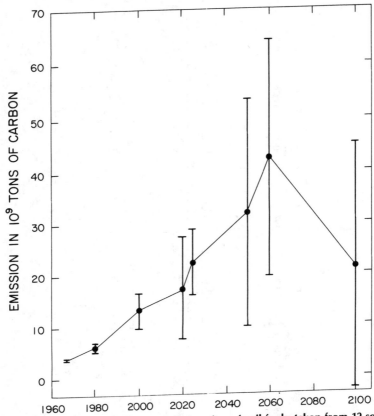

**Figure A.2.** Estimates of future CO₂ emissions from fossil fuels, taken from 12 sources. Each point and bar (mean and mean deviation) for a given year is based on at least 5 entries (prepared by E. Friedman). Sources: Rotty (1977), SCEP (1970), Keeling (1973), Zimen et al. (1977), Rotty (1973), Keeling and Bacastow (1977), Niehaus (1976), Niehaus and Williams (1979), Perry and Landsberg (1977), Voss and Niehaus (1977), Rotty (1979a), Rotty (1979b).

## 2. Future Global Carbon Dioxide Projections

Even though carbon dioxide emissions are generally expected to grow until about 2050, energy experts expect emissions to have dropped by 2100, because new nonfossil energy sources will probably be in use and because many fossil fuel resources will be nearly depleted by that time.

Figure A.2 compares the average of 12 estimates of carbon dioxide release for various years in the future, and the variation of that average. In order to provide meaningful statistics, the only years indicated are

Table A.3. Mix of fuel use and carbon emissions. Rates for these various fuel sources reflect possible future energy policies of the United States as they would apply in 1990 (Greeley, 1979).

| Energy Policy or Program | Year | Fuel Mix (%)/Carbon release ($10^9$ tons) | | | | | | | Energy Consumption (Terrawatt-yrs.) | Emissions ($10^9$ tons) | |
| --- | --- | --- | --- | --- | --- | --- | --- | --- | --- | --- | --- |
| | | Nuclear | Solar | Hydro | Coal | Synthetics* | Gas | Oil | | Carbon** | $CO_2$ |
| Present | 1975 | 2.9/0 | — | 4.2/0 | 19.8/0.35 | — | 28.2/0.29 | 45.1/0.64 | 2.38 | 1.29 | 4.73 |
| Baseline | 1990 | 9.3/0 | — | 2.8/0 | 22.8/0.61 | — | 18.7/0.29 | 46.7/1.0 | 3.58 | 1.90 | 6.96 |
| National Energy Acts | 1990 | 9.3/0 | — | 3.0/0 | 28.9/0.73 | — | 19.2/0.28 | 39.6/0.80 | 3.38 | 1.81 | 6.63 |
| Oil Decontrol / Solar Messages | 1990 | 9.3/0 | 0.6/0 | 3.0/0 | 26.8/0.68 | — | 20.9/0.31 | 39.4/0.8 | 3.39 | 1.79 | 6.54 |
| Synthetic Fuels Message | 1990 | 9.5/0 | 2.0/0 | 3.0/0 | 31.6/0.81 | 5.1/0.16 | 22.1/0.32 | 31.8/0.63 | 3.31 | 1.76 | 6.58 |

* Included in Coal figure
** Using these Conversions:  Coal: 0.75 x $10^9$ tons per terrawatt-year
Gas: 0.43 x $10^9$ tons per terrawatt-year
Oil: 0.60 x $10^9$ tons per terrawatt-year

**Table A.4.** Fraction of carbon emissions (%) by developed and developing countries, 1950–1976. Values were derived from United Nations fuel use tables (UN, 1979).

| Year | Global Emissions ($10^9$ tons Carbon) | Developed* | Developing** |
|------|---------------------------------------|------------|--------------|
| 1950 | 1.57 | 93 | 7 |
| 1951 | 1.71 | 92 | 8 |
| 1952 | 1.74 | 91 | 9 |
| 1953 | 1.79 | 91 | 9 |
| 1954 | 1.83 | 90 | 10 |
| 1955 | 2.01 | 90 | 10 |
| 1956 | 2.12 | 90 | 10 |
| 1957 | 2.19 | 89 | 11 |
| 1958 | 2.30 | 86 | 14 |
| 1959 | 2.42 | 82 | 18 |
| 1960 | 2.59 | 81 | 19 |
| 1961 | 2.53 | 85 | 15 |
| 1962 | 2.66 | 86 | 14 |
| 1963 | 2.82 | 86 | 14 |
| 1964 | 2.96 | 85 | 15 |
| 1965 | 3.09 | 85 | 15 |
| 1966 | 3.26 | 84 | 16 |
| 1967 | 3.28 | 86 | 14 |
| 1968 | 3.51 | 85 | 15 |
| 1969 | 3.74 | 85 | 15 |
| 1970 | 3.93 | 84 | 16 |
| 1971 | 4.06 | 84 | 16 |
| 1972 | 4.24 | 83 | 17 |
| 1973 | 4.46 | 83 | 17 |
| 1974 | 4.47 | 82 | 18 |
| 1975 | 4.51 | 81 | 19 |
| 1976 | 4.76 | 81 | 19 |

\* Includes centrally planned Europe
\*\* Includes centrally planned Asia

those for which at least five estimates were available. The year 1967 has also been included to provide both historical baseline and an indication of the range of predictions typical of a year in the past. A gradual increase in the range of the projections is also evident, suggesting that our confidence in them should decrease as they are extended further into the future.

## 3. Emissions by the U.S.

Although they include widely diverse energy options, the energy policies of the U.S., as defined in a series of programs promoted by the

Carter Administration, will have little effect on carbon dioxide emissions.

Computation of the carbon dioxide emissions from an energy plan is straightforward, except in the case where synthetic fuels are included. This is because the synthetic fuel would be derived from coal, unconventional fossil fuel sources (such as geopressured gas regions, tar sands, or oil shale), or from biomass. The calculations in Table A.3 take these factors into consideration. Only a slight difference in emissions can be found when comparing the last three major energy programs in the table. The synthetic fuel program, for example, would produce the equivalent of 2.5 million barrels of oil per day by 1990, but would only reduce emissions about 5 percent relative to a "baseline" case. This program would be about average in emissions relative to the two other major energy proposals.

Because manufacturing synthetic fuels produces more carbon dioxide per unit of energy than its direct counterparts, an extensive use of coal for synthetic fuels on a worldwide scale would increase carbon dioxide emissions, assuming energy demand remained the same. However, as pointed out in Sections III.2 and IV.2, coal is unevenly distributed among the countries of the world; it is unlikely that poorer countries will be able to afford large synthetic fuel programs.

## 4. Relative Emissions by Developed and Developing Countries

In Section IV.5 and elsewhere the subject of the relative contribution of carbon dioxide to the atmosphere by developed and developing countries was raised. The point of view expressed in this report is that when considering who should bear the responsibility of climate change, the *cumulative* quantity of carbon dioxide over the years is what should be taken into account instead of the emissions now or at some time in the future.

Table A.4 gives emission data up to 1976. Data since 1950 appear to be more reliable than information for earlier periods. When considering cumulative emissions it is probably adequate to assume a 4 percent per year global growth rate of fossil fuel use and carbon dioxide emissions from 1900 up to 1976. This corresponds to a doubling time of about 17 years. Figure IV.3 is based on these figures.

# REFERENCES

Darmstadter, J., and S. Schurr, 1974: World energy resources and demand. *Phil. Trans. Roy. Soc. London A276*, No. 1261, 413.

Greeley, R.S., 1979: *Analysis of National Energy Plans.* MITRE Corporation Publication MTR–79W00356, McLean, Va.

Keeling, C.D., 1973: Industrial production of carbon dioxide from fossil fuels and limestone. *Tellus* 25, 174–198.

Keeling, C.D. and R.B. Bacastow, 1977: Impact of industrial gases on climate. In *Energy and Climate*, National Academy of Sciences, Washington, D.C., 72–95.

Niehaus, F., 1976: A nonlinear eight level tandem model to calculate the future $CO_2$ and $C^{14}$ burden to the atmosphere. IIASA Res. Memo. RM–76–35, International Institute for Applied Systems Analysis, Laxenburg, Austria.

Niehaus, F. and J. Williams, 1979: Studies of different energy strategies in terms of their effects on the atmospheric $CO_2$ concentration. *J. Geophys. Res.* 84, 3123–3129.

Perry, H. and H. Landsberg, 1977: Projected world energy consumption. In *Energy and Climate*, National Academy of Sciences, Washington, D.C., 35–50.

Rotty, R.M., 1973: Commentary on and extension of calculative procedure for $CO_2$ production. *Tellus* 25, 508–516.

Rotty, R.M., 1977: Global carbon dioxide production from fossil fuels and cement, A.D. 1950 – A.D. 2000. In *The Fate of Fossil Fuel $CO_2$ in the Oceans*, N.R. Anderson, and A. Malaholf (eds.), Plenum, New York, 167–181.

Rotty, R.M., 1978: The atmospheric $CO_2$ consequences of heavy dependence on coal. In *Carbon Dioxide, Climate and Society*, J. Williams (ed.), Pergamon Press, New York.

Rotty, R.M., 1979a: (Material presented before Congress) In *Carbon Dioxide Accumulation in the Atmosphere, Synthetic Fuels and Energy Policy – A Symposium*, Committee on Governmental Affairs, U.S. Senate, Washington, D.C., July 185–194.

Rotty, R.M., 1979b: Uncertainties associated with global effects of atmospheric carbon dioxide. Institute for Energy Analysis, Oak

Ridge Associated Universities, IEA–79–6(0), Oak Ridge, Tenn., March.

SCEP, 1970: *Man's Impact on the Global Environment: Report of the Study of Critical Environmental Problems.* M.I.T. Press, Cambridge, Mass., 289–305.

Steinberg, M., A.S. Albanese and V.D. Dang, 1978: Environmental control technology for carbon dioxide. Presented at the 71st Annual Meeting of the American Institute of Chemical Engineers, November.

United Nations, 1979: *World Energy Supplies.* Statistical Papers, Series J, Dept. of International Economic and Social Affairs, Statistical Office, United Nations, New York.

Voss, A. and F. Niehaus, 1977: Die Zukunft des Weltenergie systems. *Umschau* Heft 19, 625–632.

Woodwell, G.A., G.J. MacDonald and C.D. Keeling, 1979: The carbon dioxide report. *Bull. Atomic Scientists*, October, 56–57.

Zimen, K.E., P. Offermann and G. Hartmann, 1977: Source functions of $CO_2$ and the future $CO_2$ burden in the atmosphere. *Zeits. Naturforschung* 32a, 1544–1554.

# APPENDIX B

# RESULTS OF EXPERIMENTS WITH CLIMATE MODELS

There have been a number of experiments in which coupled GCM–type atmosphere–ocean models have been run to determine the response of the model to a doubling (or quadrupling) of carbon dioxide (see Section II.3). The WMO ad hoc Study Group of the Working Group on Atmospheric Carbon Dioxide (WMO, 1979) reviewed the results of eight such experiments (one of which is invalid for reasons explained below), and the following Table B.1 summarizes the main features of each model and the general results.

**Table B.1.** Summary of climate model experiments and main features of each climate model (WMO, 1979).

| Institution and Principle Investigators | Main Features of the Model | Summary of Results of Experiments for $2 \times [CO_2]$ |
|---|---|---|
| GFDL Manabe and Wetherald (1975) | Atmosphere-ocean ("swamp") Atmospheric GCM with 9-levels, specified cloudiness, annual average insolation Ocean noncirculating, no heat capacity ("swamp" model) One idealized continent, truncated at 81°, in a 120° sector | 2.9° $\Delta \bar{T}_s$; $\Delta T_s$ as function of latitude, with 10° at highest latitude |
| GFDL Manabe and Stouffer (1979) | Atmosphere-ocean (mixed layer) Atmospheric GCM with 9 levels in vertical, specified cloudiness, seasonal insolation Ocean mixed layer (fixed 68.5m depth), noncirculating, sea ice submodel Realistic continents, mountains, global | 2° $\Delta \bar{T}_s$; $\Delta T_s$ as function of latitude and season, with high northern latitude warming of 5°–8° in winter, 2° in summer |

| | | |
|---|---|---|
| GFDL<br>Manabe and<br>Wetherald<br>(1980) | Atmosphere-ocean (swamp)<br>Atmospheric GCM with 9 levels,<br>  variable cloudiness, annual<br>  average insolation, hydrologic<br>  cycle<br>Ocean swamp model<br>One idealized continent in a 120°<br>  sector | $3°$ $\Delta \bar{T}_s$; $\Delta T_s$ as<br>function of<br>latitude, with<br>$8°$ at 80°N<br>latitude<br>Gives precip. and<br>soil moisture<br>over land |
| GFDL<br>Wetherald<br>and Manabe<br>(1980) | Atmosphere-ocean (mixed layer)<br>Atmospheric GCM with 9 levels,<br>  specified cloudiness, seasonal<br>  insolation, hydrologic cycle<br>Ocean mixed layer (fixed 68.5m depth),<br>  noncirculating, sea ice submodel<br>One idealized continent in a 120°<br>  sector | $2.4°$ $\Delta \bar{T}_s$; $\Delta T_s$ as<br>function of<br>latitude and<br>season, with<br>larger seasonal<br>amplitude at<br>high N latitude<br>in winter than<br>in summer |
| GISS<br>Hansen<br>(1979) | Atmosphere-ocean (swamp)<br>Atmospheric GCM with 7 levels,<br>  variable cloudiness, annual<br>  average insolation<br>Ocean swamp model<br>Realistic continents, mountains,<br>  global | $3.9°$ $\Delta \bar{T}_s$; larger<br>$\Delta T_s$ at high<br>latitude |
| GISS<br>Hansen<br>(1978) | Atmosphere-ocean (mixed layer)<br>Same as above, but with seasonal<br>  insolation<br>Ocean mixed layer (70m), non-<br>  circulating | $3.5°$ $\Delta \bar{T}_s$; larger<br>$\Delta T_s$ at high<br>latitude |
| OSU<br>Gates<br>(1979) | Noncoupled atmosphere-ocean<br>Atmospheric GCM with 2 levels,<br>  variable cloudiness, seasonal<br>  insolation, hydrologic cycle<br>Ocean surface temperature distribu-<br>  tion set at present values as<br>  function of season<br>Realistic continents, mountains,<br>  global | $0.3°$ $\Delta \bar{T}_s$; but<br>with SST fixed<br>this can only<br>represent a kind<br>of lower limit |
| LLL<br>MacCracken<br>and Potter<br>(1979) | Atmosphere-ocean (mixed layer)<br>Atmosphere statistical-dynamical<br>  model, 9 levels, zonally<br>  averaged, annually averaged<br>  insolation, parameterized<br>  cloudiness<br>Relative areas of continents and<br>  oceans considered in each lati-<br>  tude band, prescribed meridional<br>  heat transport in oceans | $1.5°$ $\Delta \bar{T}_s$; $2.3°$ $\Delta T_s$<br>in NH, $<1°$ $\Delta T_s$ in<br>SH |

Symbols employed in the table are as follows:
$T_s$–surface temperature; $\Delta \bar{T}_s$– globally averaged surface temperature change; SST–sea
surface temperature; NH, SH–northern, southern hemisphere.

As mentioned in Section II.3, the Oregon State University experiment with fixed ocean temperatures should not be factored in with the others, since a lower boundary condition covering four-fifths of the globe (the oceans) that shows no response is clearly unrealistic.

The National Academy of Sciences Woods Hole study (NAS, 1979) and others have speculated that the effective depth of the upper ocean that will respond to a gradual climatic change could be as much as an order of magnitude larger than the 70 meters or so that responds to seasonal changes. This is due in part to vertical mixing of water in the upper part of the thermocline in the centers of the subtropical gyres, and also to winter time deep convection at high latitudes. In any case, the larger thermal inertia of the oceans may introduce a lag of a decade, possibly two, in the process of climatic change; the change will still take place, but will occur later.

This lag effect is receiving attention now, and will complicate the simulation of the effects of increasing carbon dioxide, an increase that is also expected to occur over many decades. For one thing, the experiments described above assume a steady state condition, that is, no change of carbon dioxide during the experiment and the ocean in thermal equilibrium with the atmosphere. Since such a steady state will in fact hardly ever be attained, we must consider how to take into account the lag due to the thermal inertia of the oceans in future experiments (Schneider and Thompson, 1980).

# REFERENCES

Gates, W.L., 1979: Private communication.

GISS, 1978: *Proposal for Research in Global Carbon Dioxide Source /
Sink Budget and Climate Effects*. Goddard Inst. for Space
Studies, New York 10025 (Reported in NAS, 1979).

Hansen, J.E., 1979: Private communication (Reported in NAS, 1979; in
preparation for *J. Atmos. Sci.*).

MacCracken, M.C., and G.L. Potter, 1979: Private communication.

Manabe, S., and R. Stouffer, 1979: Study of climatic impact of $CO_2$
increase with a mathematical model of global climate. *Nature*
282, 491–493.

Manabe S., and R.T. Wetherald, 1975: The effects of doubling the $CO_2$
concentration on the climate of a general circulation model. *J.
Atmos. Sci.* 32, 3–15.

Manabe, S., and R.T. Wetherald, 1980: On the distribution of climate
change resulting from an increase in $CO_2$ content of the
atmosphere. *J. Atmos. Sci.* 37, 99–118.

NAS, 1979: *Carbon Dioxide and Climate: A Scientific Assessment*. Report
of ad hoc Study Group on Carbon Dioxide and Climate, Woods
Hole, Mass. Climate Research Board, National Academy of
Sciences, Washington, D.C.

Schneider, S.H., and S.L. Thompson, 1980: Atmospheric $CO_2$ and
climate: Importance of the transient response. *J. Geophys. Res.*
(in press).

Wetherald, R.T., and S. Manabe, 1980: Influence of seasonal variation
upon the sensitivity of a model climate. *J. Geophys. Res.* (in
press).

WMO, 1979: *Report of the Meeting of CAS Working Group on
Atmospheric Carbon Dioxide*. Boulder, Colo., November, 1979,
WMO Proj. on Res. and Monitoring of $CO_2$ Rept. No. 2, World
Meteorological Organization, Geneva. (See Appendix C of
Report No. 2).

# APPENDIX C

# Sources of Information for Climate Scenarios

In Section II.4 we discussed developing a set of scenarios showing the future climate of a warmer Earth. As we noted, there are several sources of information on which to base these scenarios, and in some cases they do not agree. Nevertheless, in Figure II.3 we attempted to draw a map of the world showing the regions where it may be wetter or drier than now during the growing season of a future warmer climate.

The sources of information on which this scenario was based are discussed here. Results of several pertinent studies are presented in the form of maps so that they can be readily compared. Some interested reader may be tempted to reinterpret the information and draw his or her own scenario.

## 1. The Altithermal (Hypsithermal) Period

Since it was published in a World Meteorological Organization Technical Note, Kellogg's 1977 map of the Altithermal Period, which occurred roughly 4500 to 8000 years ago, has been reproduced in a variety of publications (see Figure C.1). It was based on a fairly extensive but undoubtedly incomplete survey of the literature on the climate of this period; during the Altithermal the Earth was generally several degrees warmer than the present, and this map emphasizes "dryness" and "wetness" relative to the present.

Part of the evidence concerning moisture consisted of data on the kinds of plants that were growing during this period. These data were deduced from the distribution of pollen types and spores found in ancient lakes and peat bog sediments. Hence, it is probably fair to conclude that the vegetation was controlled largely by rainfall and soil moisture during the growing season (Lamb, 1977; Nichols, 1975). In middle and high latitudes this would be in the early summer months.

Another source of information on average rainfall conditions during the Altithermal is the reconstructed record of lake levels and stream flows, especially in parts of Africa (Nicholson and Flohn, 1980; Street and

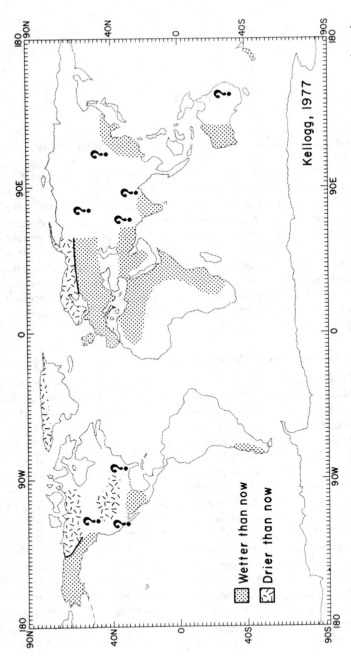

**Figure C.1.** A reconstruction of the Altithermal (or Hypsithermal) Period of about 4500 to 8000 years ago, showing areas where the conditions were wetter or drier than now. The blank areas are not necessarily regions where no change occurred; our information is incomplete (Kellogg, 1977).

Kellogg, 1977

Wetter than now

Drier than now

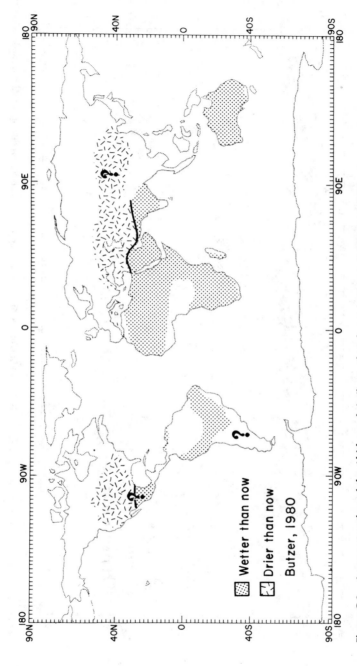

**Figure C.2.** A reconstruction of the Altithermal similar to that shown in Figure C.1 (Butzer, 1980).

Wetter than now

Drier than now

Butzer, 1980

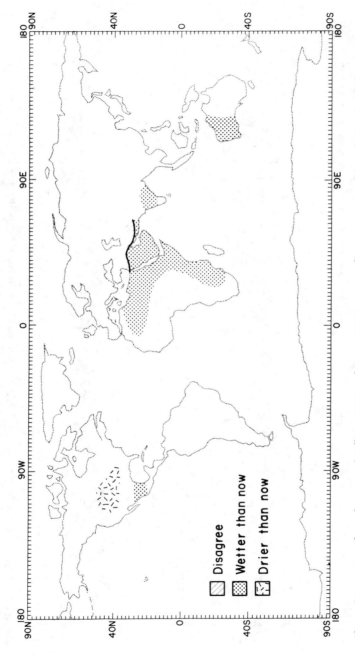

**Figure C.3.** Areas where the maps of Kellogg (1977) and Butzer (1980) agree or disagree as to conditions during the Altithermal Period.

Grove, 1976; Butzer et al, 1972). In the tropics the rainy season tends to be in the spring and summer, depending on the influence of the Asian monsoon.

A more recent study of the Altithermal Period, stimulated by Kellogg's, has been published by Butzer (1980). In Butzer's original map the "wetter" and "drier" regions are displayed, and also regions where it was significantly "warmer." The latter cover virtually all of the continents of the Northern Hemisphere north of 45°N latitude. We have replotted Butzer's data onto the same base map as Kellogg's for ease of comparison, but have not included the areas which he indicated as warmer. The result is shown in Figure C.2.

In Figure C.3 we have indicated the areas where Butzer and Kellogg agree on the change. Central North America seems to have been definitely drier during most of the Altithermal, whereas there is good evidence suggesting it was wetter in Mexico, most of north and east Africa, India (except for the southern tip), and west Australia. In our scenario map, Figure II.3, we have outlined these areas with dashed lines to mark where the changes have a somewhat higher probability of occurring as indicated.

## 2. The Modern Meteorological Record

It was suggested at a workshop sponsored by the Aspen Institute (Aspen, 1978) that one way to gain insight into how regional conditions would change on a warmer Earth would be to study years when it was unusually warm in the northern polar regions. If it turned out that warmer-than-average years had characteristic deviations in their circulation, temperature, and precipitation patterns, then these patterns might "resemble the normal climate regime of the warmed future." The Aspen report (1978) notes that the time scale of these departures from the present norm are an order of magnitude less than those of an Earth slowly warmed by the greenhouse effect. Furthermore, "the causes of (recent) past climate extremes are different from the expected carbon dioxide forcing of climate change," according to the report. Nevertheless, despite these caveats the workshop recommended that such an analysis be conducted.

Two sets of researchers independently began this study: J. Williams, then at the National Center for Atmospheric Research (Williams, 1979), and T. Wigley, P. Jones, and P. Kelly of the Climatic Research Unit, University of East Anglia (Wigley et al, 1979). The two studies differed somewhat in the assumptions made and the approaches taken; therefore the results differed as well.

161

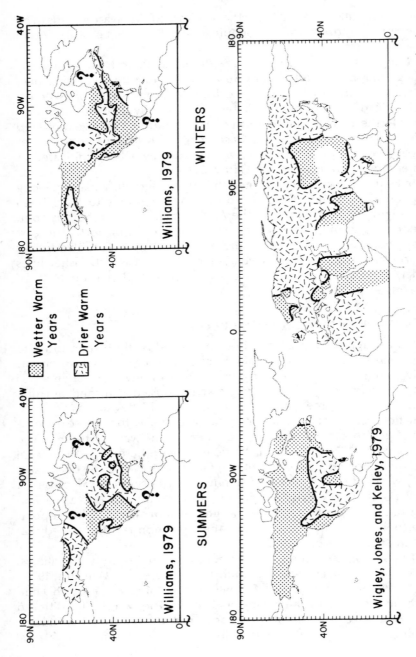

**Figure C.4.** Average deviations from the long term mean precipitation of the 10 warmest Arctic summers and 10 warmest Arctic winters (Williams, 1979); and average deviations from the long term annual mean precipitation of the 5 warmest years at 65° to 85°N latitude (Wigley et al, 1979).

162

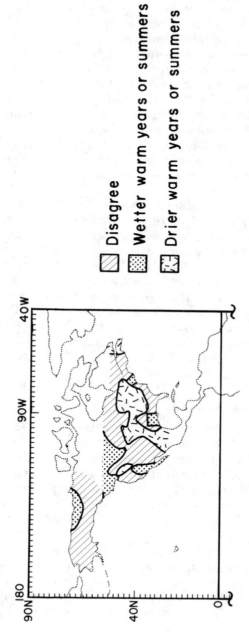

**Figure C.5.** Areas where the maps of **Williams (1979)** and **Wigley, et al., (1979)** agree as to deviations from the long term mean precipitation over North America. Williams' results apply to the summertime, whereas Wigley et al., apply to annual means.

Disagree

Wetter warm years or summers

Drier warm years or summers

Williams used 70 years of meteorological data for the Northern Hemisphere. She drew maps of the differences between the long term seasonal means for pressure, temperature, and precipitation and the 10 warmest Arctic winters and ten warmest Arctic summers. She presented the pressure and temperature departures for the entire hemisphere, but for precipitation Williams confined her analysis to the North American sector. She concluded that there were large areas of increase and decrease of precipitation, and that in the summer these were statistically significant. Her results are shown in the upper part of Figure C.4. The area of significant decrease of summertime precipitation in the Midwest roughly corresponds with the only area in North America where she found a temperature increase of more than 1°C in summer for the same sets of years — that is, temperature and precipitation are inversely correlated.

The Wigley et al. analysis used a somewhat shorter data period than Williams — 50 years instead of 70. They presented the patterns of differences between the 50-year mean and annual averages of temperature and precipitation for the five warmest years as measured in the latitutde band between 65°N and 80°N. Their results for deviations of precipitation in the Northern Hemisphere are shown in the lower part of Figure C.4. Figure C.5 shows that Wigley et al. found the same below average precipitation (and above average temperatures) in the Midwest as did Williams. However, this figure also illustrates that elsewhere in North America there is considerable disagreement, part of which may be accounted for by the fact that Williams' results for summer are being compared to Wigley et al.'s annual averages.

## 3. Climate Model Experiments

As discussed in Section II.3 and summarized in Appendix B, there have been several climate model experiments that have tried to determine the effect of a carbon dioxide doubling. The climate models have generally involved two kinds of ocean models coupled to a general circulation model (GCM) of the atmosphere: a mixed layer ocean model that permits seasonal changes to be studied, and a "swamp" model of the ocean which can only be run with annually averaged incoming solar radiation, or insolation.

At the Geophysical Fluid Dynamics Laboratory (GFDL) in Princeton both kinds of models have been run with the assumption that there is just one continent and no mountains, and with a hydrologic cycle that permits a study of precipitation, evaporation, and soil moisture over that continent. Results have been summarized by Manabe and Wetherald

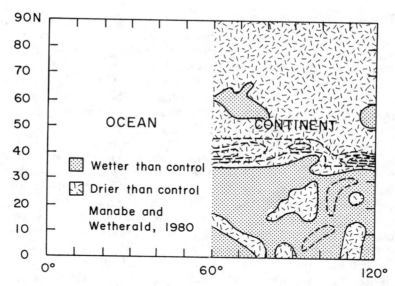

**Figure C.6.**   Soil moisture deviations from the control run of a climate model with annual average insolation when the carbon dioxide was doubled (Manabe and Wetherald, 1980).

(1980) and Wetherald and Manabe (1980); a map of the annually averaged soil moisture distribution from the former reference is shown in Figure C.6. It can be seen that a band of low soil moisture extends across the idealized continent between about 35° and 50° latitude, the maximum decrease being about 5 centimeters of water. This area of decrease of soil moisture can be attributed to the fact that the model's evaporation increased more than its precipitation for the warmer situation with doubled carbon dioxide.

When the climate model experiment with a mixed layer ocean was run to determine the change of conditions with season for a carbon dioxide doubling (Wetherald and Manabe, 1980), it was found that the maximum decrease of soil moisture at mid-latitudes occurred during the winter, spring, and early summer. The band of dryness in this model experiment shifted poleward during this period. Another area of significant dryness in this model experiment appeared poleward of 60° during the early summer months. It should be noted that the dry period at both middle and high latitudes occurred during the season when adequate soil moisture is most needed by plants.

## 4. The Soil Moisture Scenario

In drawing the soil moisture map shown in Figure II.3, we were most strongly influenced by the evidence from the Altithermal Period. That is partly because the data are more complete than for the other sources, and because the several thousand year time scale of the Altithermal was long enough to establish a sort of climatic equilibrium — though there were shorter periods during the Altithermal when anomalous conditions apparently persisted for several centuries.

However, paleoclimatic reconstructions of the Altithermal have so far given relatively little information on what happened in north and central Asia, and in parts of South America (Butzer, 1980). Arguing by analogy with what happened in Africa, which has been extensively studied, we can surmise that there may have been a small decrease on other continents along the equator and an increase in the sub-tropics (especially in regions affected by the Asian monsoon circulation). There is some indication that the western parts of North America and Europe were wetter at middle and high latitudes, but otherwise all lines of evidence, including the climate model experiments, point to a general decrease in soil moisture at those latitudes.

These are the considerations that went into the drawing of Figure II.3. Clearly a great deal more information will be needed before we can be confident that this possible scenario is indeed a credible forecast of things to come. Furthermore, we have concentrated on soil moisture, which is most important as a determinant of how plants will thrive. Temperature changes should also be derived on a regional basis, as should the variability of the weather. (We argue in Section II.4 that variability may decrease, but this is still open to debate.) And in this discussion we have said nothing about the cryosphere and a possible increase in sea level — a somewhat separate subject, but one of great significance.

# REFERENCES

Aspen, 1978: *The Consequences of a Hypothetical World Climate Scenario Based on an Assumed Global Warming Due to Increased Carbon Dioxide.* Report of Symposium and Workshop, Aspen Institute for Humanistic Studies, Boulder, Colorado.

Butzer, K. W., 1980: Adaptation to global environmental change. *Professional Geographer 32*, 269-278.

Butzer, K. E., G. L. Isaac, J. L. Richardson, and C. Washbourn-Kammau, 1972: Radiocarbon dating of East African lake levels. *Science 175*, 1069-1075.

Kellogg, W. W., 1977: *Effects of Human Activities on Global Climate.* WMO Tech. Note No. 156, World Meteorological Organization, Geneva, Switzerland.

Lamb, H. H., 1977: *Climate: Present Past and Future, Vol. 2.* Methuen, London. (See Part III.)

Manabe, S., and R. T. Wetherald, 1980: On the distribution of climate change resulting from an increase in $CO_2$ content of the atmosphere. *J. Atmos. Sci. 37*, 99-118.

Nichols, H., 1975: *Palynological and Paleoclimatic Study of the Late Quarternary Displacement of the Boreal Forest-Tundra Ecotone in Keewatin and Mackenzie, N.W.T., Canada.* Institute of Arctic and Alpine Research, Occasional Paper No. 15, Boulder, Colo.

Nicholson, S. E., and H. Flohn, 1980: African environmental and climatic changes and the general atmospheric circulation in Late Pleistocene and Holocene. *Climatic Change 2*, 313-348.

Street, F. A., and A. T. Grove, 1976: Environmental and climatic implications of Late Quaternary lake-level fluctuations in Africa. *Nature 261*, 285-390.

Wetherald, R. T., and S. Manabe, 1980: Influence of seasonal variation upon the sensitivity of a climate model. *J. Geophys. Res.* (in press).

Wigley, T.M.E., P. D. Jones and P. M. Kelly, 1979: Scenario for a warm, high-$CO_2$ world. *Nature 283*, 17-20.

Williams J., 1979: Anomalies in temperature and rainfall during warm Arctic seasons as a guide to the formulation of climate scenarios. *Climatic Change 2*, 249-266.

# INDEX